AF271819

EUL VERLAG

SCHRIFTEN ZU KOOPERATIONS- UND MEDIENSYSTEMEN

Herausgegeben von Prof. Dr. Volker Wulf, Siegen, Prof. Dr. Jörg Haake, Hagen, Prof. Dr. Thomas Herrmann, Bochum, Prof. Dr. Helmut Krcmar, München, Prof. Dr. Johann Schlichter, München, Prof. Dr. Gerhard Schwabe, Zürich, und Prof. Dr.-Ing. Jürgen Ziegler, Duisburg

Band 29
Michael Prilla
Wissensmanagement-Unterstützung für die Entwicklung und Nutzung von Prozessmodellen als wissensvermittelnde Artefakte
Lohmar – Köln 2010 ◆ 424 S. ◆ € 67,- (D) ◆ ISBN 978-3-89936-966-3

Band 30
Joachim Hafkesbrink, H. Ulrich Hoppe und Johann Schlichter (Hrsg.)
Competence Management for Open Innovation – Tools and IT support to unlock the innovation potential beyond company boundaries
Lohmar – Köln 2010 ◆ 336 S. ◆ € 63,- (D) ◆ ISBN 978-3-8441-0002-0

Band 31
Jan Marco Leimeister, Helmut Krcmar, Michael Koch und Kathrin Möslein (Hrsg.)
Gemeinschaftsgestützte Innovationsentwicklung für Softwareunternehmen
Lohmar – Köln 2011 ◆ 452 S. ◆ € 69,- (D) ◆ ISBN 978-3-8441-0092-1

Band 32
Ayşegül Doğangün
Adaptive Awareness-Assistenten – Entwicklung und empirische Untersuchung der Wirksamkeit
Lohmar – Köln 2012 ◆ 268 S. ◆ € 57,- (D) ◆ ISBN 978-3-8441-0187-4

Band 33
Fan Bai
Collaboration Support for the Distributed Development of Ontologies
Lohmar – Köln 2013 ◆ 140 S. ◆ € 43,- (D) ◆ ISBN 978-3-8441-0228-4

JOSEF EUL VERLAG

COLLABORATION SUPPORT FOR THE
DISTRIBUTED DEVELOPMENT OF ONTOLOGIES

From the Faculty of Engineering

Department of Computer and Cognitive Sciences

of University Duisburg-Essen

for the acquisition of the academic degree

Doctor of Engineering

approved Dissertation

from

Fan.Bai

from Shanghai

1. Appraise: Prof Dr.-Ing. Juergen Ziegler
2. Appraise: Prof Dr. Heinz Ulrich Hoppe
   The day of comprehensive examination: 21. Juni 2012

Schriften zu Kooperations- und Mediensystemen · Band 33
Herausgegeben von Prof. Dr. Volker Wulf, Siegen, Prof. Dr. Jörg Haake,
Hagen, Prof. Dr. Thomas Herrmann, Bochum, Prof. Dr. Helmut Krcmar,
München, Prof. Dr. Johann Schlichter, München, Prof. Dr. Gerhard
Schwabe, Zürich, und Prof. Dr.-Ing. Jürgen Ziegler, Duisburg

Fan Bai

Collaboration Support for the Distributed Development of Ontologies

With a Foreword by Prof. Dr.-Ing. Jürgen Ziegler,
Universität Duisburg-Essen

EUL VERLAG

Bibliografische Information der Deutschen Nationalbibliothek

Die Deutsche Nationalbibliothek verzeichnet diese Publikation
in der Deutschen Nationalbibliografie; detaillierte bibliografische
Daten sind im Internet über <http://dnb.d-nb.de> abrufbar.

Dissertation, Universität Duisburg-Essen, 2012

ISBN 978-3-8441-0228-4
1. Auflage Februar 2013

© JOSEF EUL VERLAG GmbH, Lohmar – Köln, 2013
Alle Rechte vorbehalten

Umschlaggestaltung: Luzia Sassen

JOSEF EUL VERLAG GmbH
Brandsberg 6
53797 Lohmar
Tel.: 0 22 05 / 90 10 6-6
Fax: 0 22 05 / 90 10 6-88
E-Mail: info@eul-verlag.de
http://www.eul-verlag.de

**Bei der Herstellung unserer Bücher möchten wir die Umwelt schonen. Dieses
Buch ist daher auf säurefreiem, 100% chlorfrei gebleichtem, alterungsbestän-
digem Papier nach DIN 6738 gedruckt.**

Foreword

In the course of the decade which has passed since the vision of a Semantic Web was first articulated by Tim Berners-Lee and others, the amount of data on the Web represented with semantic techniques has increased enormously. In contrast to the conventional Web which links web pages as complete documents, the Semantic Web links data based on a uniform data model. This model consists of elementary statements in 'subject-predicate-object' form, mostly expressed with RDF, and uses shared vocabularies defined as ontologies by means of RDFS and OWL. Linking the individual statements results in single immense data graph which is often referred to as the Web of Data.

The development of shared conceptual structures and vocabularies in the form of ontologies forms one of the cornerstones for the successful application of semantic techniques. At the same time, defining high-quality ontologies and achieving consensus on them among the many stakeholders that are usually involved in such a process constitutes also a major bottleneck in the advancement of semantic technologies.

The work presented in this volume addresses one of the critical aspects in ontology development, namely to better support cooperation among distributed groups of ontology developers. The author has developed a set of novel methods for supporting cooperative development of ontologies, both in synchronous and asynchronous collaboration. An important contribution of this work is the provision of a method and a tool that allow for a fine-grained version control of ontology elements, enabling developers to work separately and asynchronously on some part of an ontology which can then be more effectively merged with the developments of the collaborators.

The methods and tools developed by the author form an important contribution to facilitating a more wide-spread use of semantic technologies, both on the Web as well as in specific applications, and thus also add to promoting the vision of the Semantic Web.

Duisburg, January 2013
Prof. Dr.-Ing. Juergen Ziegler

Preface

The dissertation presented in this volume introduces methods and techniques for developing a collaborative ontology development environment. With a focus on supporting synchronous cooperation, several functions have been implemented inside the Ontoverse Editor. The editor is one of the core components of the Ontoverse research project which offers a platform to support multiple users working together to create a robust ontology. Asynchronous cooperation support was developed in an extension of the editor. Functionalities such as controlling versions of an ontology resource or tracing history were realized. The unique contribution of the dissertation is that we provided several novel asynchronous cooperation supports for ontology development by using a new mechanism to control version on a fine-grained level of ontologies- on the level of ontology resources.

Completing a dissertation is hard work and would not have been possible without the help of others. I would like to thank my supervisor, Prof. Juergen Ziegler, for lots of great inspirations, ideas, comments and an endless amendment of the dissertation. I am glad that I could work with colleagues of the Ontoverse project. They provided me with many valuable feedbacks during the implementation. Thanks also for all my fellow doctoral students for their suggestions and they did a perfect evaluation for my systems. I also thank the Collide team of the University of Duisburg-Essen for their great support in developing my system.

I could not have completed the work without support from my wife and my parents. At last, I believe that the dissertation would be a nice gift for our first baby, Kalantha Yueheng Bai, even though she is too little to speak out at the moment.

Buchholz i.d Nordheide, January 2013
Fan Bai

Abstract

Ontologies, originally introduced into the world of computer science by researchers in the field of artificial intelligence in the 1980s, aim to capture knowledge as a formal structural framework. A number of applications, including the newly emerged social network and the semantic web, utilize ontologies as their backbone.

Many stakeholders, such as domain experts, ontology experts and final users, can be involved in the ontology development procedure which may span a long period of time. Therefore it is critical for ontology developers to work at a suitable development environment which facilitates the ontology building. In the past decades, a lot of efforts are exerted on providing such environments. An efficient and effective tool has not yet to be developed, though.

In this dissertation we focus our effort on providing an easy-for-use collaborative ontology development environment for ontology developers. We firstly studied the most important features required during the ontology implementation phase. Following this study, we built the first prototype system which servers numerous functions in supporting synchronize cooperation. For example, with the help of group-awareness and a locking mechanism, involved developers become aware of actions from other users, which enables them to work without conflict in terms of editing same ontology resources.

With the know-how gathered from implementing the first prototype system, requirements of supporting asynchronous cooperation were studied. A version control system especially in the fields of coping with ontology data structure is therefore a central component to serve our purpose. As an extension of the first system, the second approach primarily supports local workspace and controls version on the level of ontology resources. Although working in their own workspace ontology developers can achieve a consensual shared ontology through committing, updating and merging activities. Each version of an ontology resource will be reserved during development in form of snapshot. The evolution of either a single ontology resource or the entire ontology can further be illustrated.

Although the overall approaches presented in this dissertation are still in the elementary phases, we proposed a couple of suggestions in the last part of the dissertation with regard to better implementation in the future.

Contents

List of Figures

List of Tables

Chapter 1

Introduction

Ontologies, originally a notion in philosophy, have in recent years become popular in the world of computer science. Researchers in the field of artificial intelligence first used the term ontology in the 1980s for describing computational models used to capture knowledge. Ontologies have been used since then as the formal structural framework in many computational fields, such as system engineering, software engineering, biomedical informatics, and library science. As newly emerged techniques in the web area, the semantic web and social networks use also ontologies as their backbone.

Ontologies generally describe the world of existence. In computer science, they specify concepts and their relations as domain knowledge using a formal representational language. Notions of concepts and their relationships build up a knowledge net in which, once provided with the proper reasoning mechanisms, the connotative meaning of a concept can be calculated based on limited input parameters.

We would like to lay out a small example here to illustrate the notion of ontology and what it can be used for. Imagine that you accidentally are asked to help your best friend look after his cat temporarily for several weeks. You have no idea what pet foods you have to buy. Your neighbors may give you the tip that you can buy a 200 g cat-food-can of the brand 'Whiskas' in the Wal-Mart located only 200 meters away from your home. To give such a tip by a computer application, however, is difficult to accomplish. The trouble is the understanding of the relation between cat and Wal-Mart from a software point of view, that is to say, that the software does not understand the *semantic* meaning of these two concepts.

When we have a knowledge model with the following information:

1. A Cat eats Cat-Food

2. Whiskas is a brand of Cat-Food

3. A Super-Market sells Cat-Food

4. Wal-Mart is a Super-Market

provided with a proper reasoning mechanism, applications could calculate the relation between the concept *Cat* and the concept *Wal-Mart* and provide a suggestion similar to that from your neighbors. Based on this model, the semantic meaning of concepts can be decided computationally and the previous *smart* tip may be suggested by a software application, such as a web-portal.

The model we described here is a type of ontology (though it is informal and unstructured). Concepts, which are nouns in the model, and their relations, which are verbs in the model, constitute the primary components of ontologies. Extended domain knowledge, such as geographic knowledge and packing knowledge, helps the application give better suggestions, for instance, to buy the 200 g can from a nearby Wal-Mart.

It is clear that such calculations can be done only if the model of the domain knowledge is correct. The more accurate and detailed the models are, the better are the results which can be obtained from the calculations. But if the scope of the knowledge covers many domains, the size of the model can be very large and there may be no standardization of the terms in the domain. Hence, building correct and detailed knowledge models is not easy. The fact that building ontologies is a type of work performed by multiple developers increases the difficulty in developing ontologies. Better cooperation during ontology development enhances the quality of ontologies. When cooperation, however, is not sufficiently supported, this may lead to confusion both in the ontology definitions and their use. To offer a better solution for collaborative ontology development is the purpose of this dissertation.

1.1 Definition and Brief History of the Term Ontology

In this section we will discuss what is an ontology and briefly introduce the history of the term. A short introduction can be found in [16].

In the 1990s the term **ontology** started to be used in the Knowledge Engineering (KB) community. One of the first definitions was given by Neches et al. [49], who defined an ontology as follows: *"an ontology defines the basic terms and relations comprising the vocabulary of a topic area as well as the rules for combining terms and relations to define extensions to the vocabulary."* This definition presents several basic notions that are widely used. It identifies the basic terms and relations between terms, identifies rules for combining terms, and provides the definitions of such terms and relations.

A few years later, Gruber provided a definition which has been quoted frequently in the literature and by the ontology community. He defined that an ontology is *"an explicit specification of a conceptualization"* [30]. A number of new definitions have been proposed, based on this definition.

Borst [10] changed slightly Gruber's definition: *"Ontologies are defined as a formal specification of a shared conceptualization."* Studer et al. [67] merged Gruber's and Borst's definitions in 1998 as follows: *"Conceptualization refers to an abstract model of some phenomenon in the world by having identified the relevant concepts of that phenomenon. Explicit means that the type of concepts used, and the constraints on their use are explicitly defined. Formal refers to the fact that the ontology should be machine readable. Shared reflects the notion that an ontology captures consensual knowledge, that is, it is not private of some individual, but accepted by a group."*

Another definition of ontology was presented, for example, in the KACTUS project [9] based on the view that developers build up ontologies by means of *extracting* the ontology from a knowledge base following a bottom-up strategy. Thus Bernaras et al. proposed their definition of an ontology as follows: *"it [an ontology] provides the means for describing explicitly the conceptualization behind the knowledge represented in a knowledge base"* [7].

The methodology used in developing the SENSUS ontology[72] follows another line of thinking. By reusing a pre-defined ontology developers can build domain specific ontologies and this alternative strategy has led to a corresponding definition: *"an ontology is a hierarchically structured set of terms for describing a domain that can be used as a skeletal foundation for a knowledge base."* In this development methodology, a large ontology can be used for building several domain KBs. New domain-specific terms can be added to the existed ontologies.

The taxonomies used by some applications which provide a consensual conceptualization of a given domain have also been considered as ontologies. These ontologies are usually defined as *lightweight* ontologies. In contrast, the term *heavyweight* ontology refers to those which provide more structure to the domain knowledge.

1.2 Collaborative Ontology Development.

Considering the definitions of the term ontology, one of the important features is that an ontology refers to shared and consensual knowledge of a domain. Straightforwardly, this definition involves cooperation during ontology building and usage. The extent and style of such cooperation depends on various aspects, e.g., the domain of the ontology, its size, the number of stakeholders, the purpose of developing the ontology, etc.

The requirement of cooperation is relevant during the entire life-cycle of an ontology, from the very first beginning of problem identification, up to the maintaining of released ontologies. Various kinds of cooperation will be performed in different steps of ontology building and using. In this section we will try to analyze these cooperative requirements and group them into different categories following the standard Computer Supported Collaborative Work (CSCW) principles. Such a study restricts the scope of our research area and leads to the goals of this dissertation.

Although there has been no general agreement on a standard ontology life-cycle so far, based on several methodologies of ontology engineering, which will be discussed in details later in the dissertation, we assume that the following steps are commonly agreed on by many ontology developers.

Start Up is the phase where the idea emerges. Why should we build the ontology? Who will use it? How to use it? These questions will be answered in this phase. In this very initial stage there is usually a limited number of people involved and synchronous cooperation is the major method. Face-to-face meetings, brain storming, voting, affinity diagramming, etc, are some representative activities.

Concept Analysis is the analysis phase where domain experts are trying to define the domain knowledge in a formalized way. Questions such as what is the definition of the concept, what are the relations among the different concepts, what is the proper name for the concept, need to be resolved. Individual knowledge of the domain, personal experience, and literal documents are typically the bases for such analysis. Domain experts coming from different areas are required to work together since overlapping knowledge helps to achieve an acceptable result. Synchronous, as well as asynchronous collaborative working activities occur in this phase, such as e-mail, on-line discussion, literature sharing and retrieving, chatting, etc.

The *Implementation Phase* is the phase where ontology experts, working with domain experts, translate the formalized definition of concepts into a knowledge representation language. GUI-based ontology development tools help ontology experts realize such a goal. Computer supported collaborative work usually plays a more important role than in the previous phases. Group awareness, what you see is what I see (WYSIWIS), version control, and private or shared workspaces, are functionality that may be useful in this phase.

The *Maintenance Phase* is the final phase where the users use the ontology in applications and, working with ontology developers, mature the ontology during use. The fact that usually ontology users are not developers themselves and are working in a different place and time is the main reason that asynchronous cooperation predominates in this phase. Information, such as bug reports and new requirements of the current ontology version, needs to be transferred asynchronously. Web forums, social networks, mailing lists, and tagging are some typical methods used in this phase.

Finding a suitable distinction between the synchronous cooperation activities and the asynchronous ones is the first step to reach our goal. To find a proper architecture and methods to support cooperation tasks, taking into account the basic architectures used in the CSCW field is helpful.

According to the principles of CSCW, there are four different categories of collaborative activities. This classification is indicated in Fig. 1.1. Different categories of collaborative working activities demand different requirements and thus leads to different decisions about choosing system architectures and implementation techniques.

	Same Place	Different Place
Same Time	SS	SD
Different Time	DS	DD

Figure 1.1: Categories according to the Principles of CSCW [3]

The activities belonging to the "same place, same time" (SS) category are very common when persons are working together in a close environment. Without barriers in time and location, involved persons are easy to communicate between each other. If an ontology is not large or if only a small group of people is dealing with a sub-task of an ontology, this category of activities is common. To support this type of cooperation activity, such as meeting, discussion, or brain storming, one of the important tasks is to help people record important information, both verbal and written, in a persistent medium so that it may be traceable for later query. The recorded information will support people in their decision making, origin tracing, etc. Databases, audio/video recordings, data-collection and sorting are often required to support these imperatives.

The " same time, different places" (SD) activities will be performed frequently when an ontology will be developed or used by people who are working not too far away from each other. Many people from different organizations and companies as well as communities will be involved in building, using and maintaining such ontology. However, this case applies when these people are working in a relatively small region and the time difference is small or none. General computer functions in this scenario try to help users communicate in an easy way and make sense of the existence and status of co-workers. Group awareness, audio/video conference, literal chatting, and WYSIWIS are standard methods for such purposes. Intranet, shared workspaces, a centralized database, as well as a centralized application server are very commonly used in implementing such methods.

Activities from the "different time, different places" (DD) scenario are common if a large number of developers and users are involved in the life-cycle of the ontology development. We could probably assume that these people come from different companies, communities, and departments, and are located in different continents of the world. Synchronized communication methods are not the main measures to support collaborative working in this scenario. The challenges to supporting such cooperation are usually harder to meet because the isolation among the developers is greater. The time difference between locations may be large and thus, because of different working times, information can not be transfered to its recipients in time. Users have to rely primarily on asynchronous communication channels and stronger control and management of the development is also required. Web based forums, version control systems, heterogeneous environment supporting tools, and social networks, are some of the feasible techniques that help people control development and ensure reliable communication channels.

The category of "different time, same place" (DS) is not common in ontology development and thus will not be discussed in details.

1.3 Goals and Structure of the Dissertation

1.3.1 Goals of the Dissertation

As discussed in previous section, a range of collaborative activities will be performed during the process of ontology development. In this dissertation we focus our interest on how to support an efficient and easy-to-use collaborative working environment for ontology developers to implement ontologies. This main goal can be decomposed into several subordinate goals.

In terms of providing a better collaborative working environment for ontology developers, the first step we need to take is to find out what kind of requirements are demanded by developers. Although the importance of collaboration during ontology development has been widely acknowledged, a clear definition of the required collaboration support in ontology development tools is still in its initial phase. To address these requirements, we studied a number of methodologies and tools which have been proposed in the literature. By studying their strong points and analyzing their insufficiencies we propose a new solution for collaborative ontology development with centralized data management.

Firstly, a synchronous and data-centralized ontology development tool has been implemented to address some common requirements in collaborative ontology development. This tool supports synchronous activity awareness and WYSIWIS. A locking mechanism is provided to control synchronous data manipulation. When working with the web-based platform, the tool supports developers working in a closely interconnected environment.

Such synchronous and data-centralized tools are commonly accepted by the ontology development communities. A number of collaborative activities can be easily supported by this configuration, such as group-awareness and chatting. Nevertheless, we noticed that an asynchronous and data-distributed structure shows its benefits in supporting some important features. One important feature among them is private workspace. Compared to the shared workspace, an individual workspace for a developer usually means a separate undisturbed environment. In this environment it is easier to hold personal views of certain domain knowledge, as compared to the data-centralized one. Another important feature is versioning. Asynchronous data manipulation and distributed data storage requires data reversion in a smaller scale. Not only does the entire ontology file need reversion, but the modification of each ontology resource should be traced and managed as well.

Based on the first tool, we developed an extension which supports asynchronous and distribted collaboration during development. Reaching a consensus in this environment is harder than with data-centralized tools. Conflicts occur easily when different developers have similar but not identical opinions on a domain concept. Merging different copies of an ontology resource is needed to get a consensual and shared representation of the knowledge. Such a working process consumes time but brings benefits. Different opinions are forced to be carefully reviewed during the merging process thus increasing the quality of the ontology. An ontology version control system helps developers working on this environment and manages the modification of each ontology resource. Finally an evaluation has been performed to analyze the effectiveness of the approach.

1.3.2   Overview of the Dissertation

The rest of this dissertation is organized as follows:

We will first study the methodologies and tools which support collaborative ontology development in Chapter 2. In this chapter, several commonly used methodologies will be introduced. The discussion focuses on the stages that users need to perform during the entire life cycle of the ontology development of each methodology. We aim at identifying tasks and actions that are commonly defined and need to be performed in order to get a robust ontology. Some tools utilized by developers help build ontologies in a collaborative fashion. We list the most popular editors and describe their features.

We conclude this part with some requirements derived from the discussion of each approach in this chapter. In Chapter 3, we compare the current editors and identify their limits and shortcomings. Based on this analysis and the previous discussion in methodologies, general requirements will be identified.

In this dissertation, we developed two prototype approaches to study how to better support collaborative ontology development. In the first system we concentrated on providing a group-awareness environment which uses a shared workspace. The editor can be used on the Web which is embedded into the Ontoverse platform. In this editor, developers can be aware of the actions and changes performed by coworkers. The editor controls the sequence of operation in order to avoid conflicts. We will discuss this approach in Chapter 4.

In the second approach, we aimed at providing better support for asynchronous development situation. In this system, each ontology developer has a private workspace and may edit the ontology in any time. Private views of a domain concept can be developed and preserved at the local client. By actions of updating, committing and merging, consensus will be reached and a shared version of concept will be stored at a central repository. The system also offers ontology version control at a high level of granularity. This tool will be introduced in Chapter 6. The method is based on decomposing an ontology into small units and controlling the synchronization of these units. By actions of committing, updating, as well as comparing and merging, a group of users can reach consensus on an ontology in a shared work space. The method and techniques of implementation as well as the visualization of the system will be discussed in details in this chapter.

In Chapter 7 we present information on the implementation of the editor in details. UML class diagrams and sequence diagrams are the primary means for describing the implementation of the system. In the last part of the dissertation, we present an initial evaluation of the version control system and conclude the dissertation by discussing the results achieved and the potential for future work.

Chapter 2

Collaborative Ontology Development Methodologies and Tools

Current research into collaborative ontology development focuses both on ontology engineering methodology and development environments. In this chapter we will look at the state-of-the-art of the methodologies and tools, analyze the their differences and shortcomings, and try to discover the general requirements for collaborative ontology developments.

2.1 Overview of Ontology Engineering

An ontology can be seen as the generic and formal expression of a body of consensual knowledge. The purpose of such an expression is so that it can be reused and shared across applications and peoples [16]. In order to make full use of the advantages that an ontology could bring, it is premised that the ontologies themselves should cover the target domain to a sufficient degree of completeness and not contain too many errors, conflicts, or inaccuracies. To build such healthy ontologies, ontology engineering was introduced to support the full life cycle of ontology development.

Ontology engineering (OE) is formally defined as "the set of activities that concern the ontology development process, the ontology life cycle, and the methodologies, tools and languages for building ontolgies" [27]. It was evolved continuously after its first appearance. Already in 1990, Lenat and Guha published the general steps [41] about Cyc development. Later in 1995, guidelines were proposed and refined in [79, 80] based on the experience gathered from [81, 31]. The methodologies METHONTOLOGY [44] and On-To-Knowledge [65] are two representative methodologies for centralized OE[63], suitable for the development of ontologies for a specific purpose within an organization: participants are usually gathered in one location and communication within the team occurs in Face-to-Face meetings. The requirement of involving ontology users in ontology creation appeared, so that the new methodologies HCOME[38] and DILIGENT[73] were introduced to meet such

9

a requirement. These methodologies take the activities of users into account so that new concepts, relations, and axioms can be duly added to the current ontologies. They are good examples of decentralized OE, which is more relevant in the Semantic Web context or other large-scale distributed environments: the team members are dispersed over several locations and affiliated to different organizations; communication is typically asynchronous; and the ontology provides a lingua franca between different stakeholders and ensures interoperability between the machines, humans, or both. The emergence of Web 2.0 assisted the ontology development based on community. Approaches based on Wikis [74], tagging [12] or casual games [64] were published.

Although there is still no standard methodology guiding the development of ontologies, general consensual agreements have been achieved. Such methodologies identify the stages during the ontology development process. The usually accepted stages are specification, conceptualization, formalization, implementation, and maintenance [59]. The main tasks and introduction of each stage are as follows:

Specification: A number of initial tasks will be performed to answer such questions as, what is the purpose of the ontology? Who will use the ontology? What domain knowledge should be covered by the ontology? The proper responses limit the scope and complexity of the ontology and lead to a successful development process and final employment.

Conceptualization: The main task of this phase is to build up a conceptual model of the domain knowledge. It describes, in a conceptual model, the ontology to be built so that it meets the specification found in the previous step. Concepts in the domain and the relationships among those concepts make up such a model. The relationships enhance stronger connections between groups of concepts. These groups of highly connected concepts usually correspond to different modules into which the domain can be decomposed.

Formalization: Developers will transform the conceptual description into a formal model, that is, the description of the domain found in the previous step is written in a more formal form, although not yet the final form. Concepts are usually defined through axioms that restrict the possible interpretations for the meaning of those concepts. Concepts are usually hierarchically organized through a structuring relation, such "is-a" and "part-of."

Implementation: The formalized domain knowledge will then be written in a knowledge representation language. For that, one commits to a representation ontology, chooses a representation language, and writes the formal model in that representation language using that representation ontology.

Maintenance: After releasing the ontology, developers are still required to perform modification of the current ontology to meet users' new demands or fix bugs. This work plays an important role in maturing the ontology.

Participants and their roles are also defined in the methodologies. Typical roles are: domain expert, user, knowledge engineer, and ontology engineer. In empirical development processes, there do not exist clear and sharp boundaries between these roles.

Instead of using the waterfall [61] and iterative [5] life-cycle models, the "evolving prototype" life-cycle model is utilized by these methodologies. In this model one can go from any activity back to any previous activity of the development process. It ensures that the ontology can be improved so long as it does not satisfy evaluation criteria or does not meet all requirements. Fig. 2.1 compares these models.

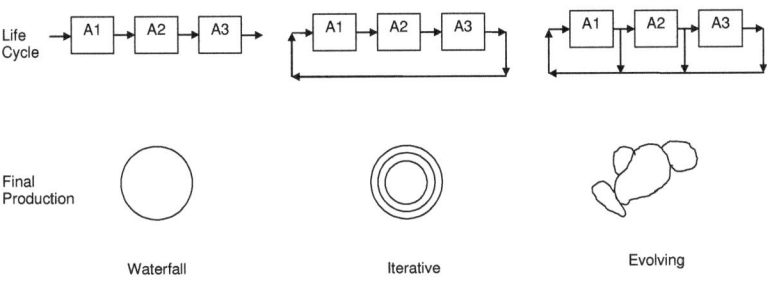

Figure 2.1: Comparison of Life Cycles [59]

The methods adopted in ontology creation may be various. Some ontologies may be created from scratch, generated from fusion, or integrated from several existing ontologies, whereas some may be partitioning from a very large existing ontology. The methodologies for each of them are correspondingly different. For example, [44, 65, 73], are representative methodologies for building ontologies from scratch. [72] discusses how to generate domain specific ontology from a large generic ontology. When several small ontologies exist, no one of which subsumes any other, developers may synthesize the traits of these base ontologies and develop a unified ontology with the help of other concepts pertaining to the described phenomenon [33, 32]. A main characteristic of ontology building is that it is a learning process and a continuous evolution will occur during the building procedure. To support such features, a model of the ontology maturing process has been proposed. [12]

2.2 Introduction of Representative Methodologies

In the previous section we gave an overview of the methodologies, that have been proposed to achieve more systematic and effective ontology engineering processes. In this section some representative methodologies will be discussed in detail. By introducing the detailed process and comparing these methodologies, the general requirements for collaborative ontology development will be deduced. As mentioned in the previous section, different methods fit for different development scenarios. This thesis will be focused on the methodologies that enable building ontologies from scratch. In this section, METHONTOLOGY, On-To-Knowledge, and DILIGENT will be discussed. Furthermore, the model of the ontology maturing process will also be discussed as a complementary approach.

2.2.1   METHONTOLOGY

METHONTOLOGY was used to build *Chemicals*, an ontology about the chemical elements of the periodic table. It was described in [44, 24]. This framework includes: the identification of the ontology development process, a life cycle based on evolving prototypes, and the methodology itself. The ontology development process identifies which tasks should be performed in building ontologies. The life cycle depicts the stages through which the ontology passes during its lifetime, as well as the interdependencies with the life cycles of other ontologies. The methodology illustrates the sequences for performing each task, the techniques used, the products to be output, and how the ontologies are to be evaluated.

The general steps of METHONTOLOGY can be divided into four steps[44]:

- Step 1. To capture knowledge of a given domain and to develop a requirement specification document.

- Step 2. To conceptualize it in a set of intermediate representations (IRs).

- Step 3. To implement the conceptual model in a formal language.

- Step 4. To evaluate the ontology with respect to a frame of reference during each phase and between phases of their life cycle [28].

Fig. 2.2 shows the ontology life cycle in this methodology.

The main phase in the ontology development process using the METHONTOLOGY approach is the conceptualization phase (Step 2). Activities and detailed IRs were identified and described as follows [44]:

1. To identify concepts, their instances, attributes and their values in a Data Dictionary.

2. To classify groups of concepts in Concept Classification Trees.

3. To describe constants in a Table of Constants.

4. To describe instance attributes and class attributes in Tables of Instance Attributes and Tables of Class Attributes

5. To describe formulas used to infer numerical values of attributes by using Tables of Formulas.

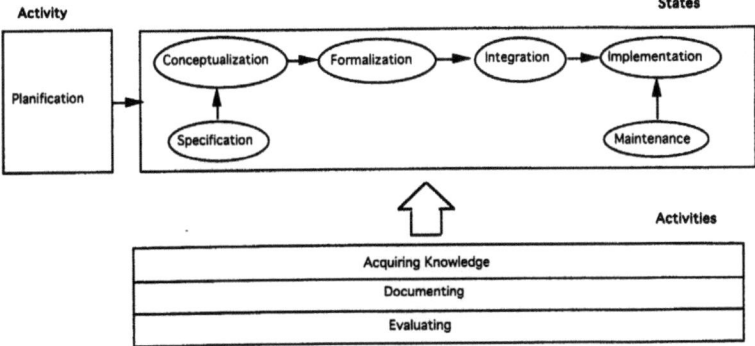

Figure 2.2: The Life Cycle of the METHONTOLOGY [24]

6. To gather the inference sequence of the attributes in Attribute Classification Trees.

7. To describe instances in Tables of Instances.

Activities 1 to 7 are not sequential in the sense of a waterfall life-cycle model, but a kind of sequentiality of some kind must be followed to assure that the first two steps lead to a well-defined model without any redundancies, omissions, or inconsistencies. At this phase, the documentation generated allows[44]:

- to figure out if an ontology is useful and usable for a given application without inspecting its source code;

- to compare the scope and completeness of several ontologies, their reusability, and shareability by analyzing the knowledge expressed in each IR.

Beside the detailed defined activities and IRs in the conceptualization phase, several knowledge acquisition techniques were also proposed: non-structured and structured interviews with experts, informal and formal text analysis, analysis of tables and graphs with relevant information about the domain, etc.

2.2.2 On-To-Knowledge

As the power of ontology is raised by providing a formal conceptualization of a particular domain that can be shared by a group of people in an organization [54], it has become an important tool for knowledge management (KM) in enterprises. The On-To-Knowledge (OTK) methodology [65] covers the range from the early stages of setting up a KM project to the final roll out of the ontology-based KM application based on an analysis of usage scenarios. In this thesis, only the development of the ontology will be taken into consideration. Similar to the METHONTOLOGY

14

methodology, this development process was divided into several stages. The relevant activities and their involved documents were also elaborated. Fig. 2.3 shows the life cycle of this methodology.

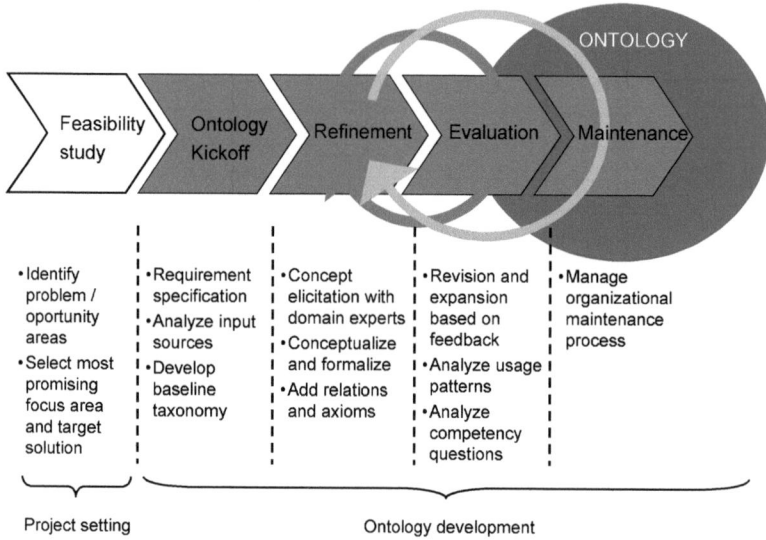

Figure 2.3: The Life Cycle of On-To-Knowledge [65]

Feasibility Study. Factors that might lead to the success or failure of a knowledge management system are not restricted to the technological. To identify problem/opportunity areas and potential solutions, and to put them into a wider organizational perspective, it is necessary to execute a feasibility study, a phase which supports decisions as to economical and technical project feasibility.

Kickoff Phase for Ontology Development. Identifying the purpose and sketching the planned final result are key points for many engineering methodologies. In this phase, ontology engineers will decide on the inclusion, exclusion and hierarchical structure of the concepts in the ontology. Meanwhile, once those existed ontologies which have been decided to be reused in the developing ontology, will be further studied. The objective is to represent a document that demonstrates the following information[65]:

1. Goal of the ontology

2. Domain and scope

3. Applications supported by the ontology

4. Knowledge sources (e.g. domain experts, organization charts, business plans, dictionaries, index lists, db-schemas, etc.)

5. Potential users and usage scenarios

6. Competency questionnaire

7. Potentially reusable ontologies

Refinement Phase. The product of this phase is a mature and application-oriented target ontology suitable to the specification given by the kickoff phase. This phase includes several sub-phases to generate the product. There are[65]:

- The gathering of an "baseline taxonomy" containing the relevant concepts given during the kickoff phase.

- A knowledge elicitation process with domain experts based on the initial input from the baseline taxonomy to develop a "seed ontology" containing the relevant concepts, relations between them, and axioms on top. The seed ontology is usually expressed at an epistemological level.

- A conceptualization and formalization phase to transfer the seed ontology into the "target ontology" expressed in formal representation languages.

Potentially reusable ontologies which were defined in the kickoff phase may give useful hints for increasing the speed and quality of the development during the refinement phase.

Evaluation Phase. The evaluation phase serves as a proof of the usefulness of the developed ontologies and their associated software environments. The ontology engineer will check firstly whether the ontology satisfies the ontology requirements specification document and whether the ontology supports the competency questions analyzed in the kickoff phase. Then the ontology engineer needs to put the ontology into the associated software environments and test the application. Feedback from beta users may help the developers generate a more mature ontology in the next iterative refinement phase, which is closely linked to the refinement phase, and ontology engineers may need to perform several cycles until the target ontology reaches the envisaged level.

Maintenance Phase. Specifications for ontologies do change in the real world. The OTK methodology is based on the assumption that the maintenance of ontologies is primarily an organizational process. Strict rules for the update–delete–insert processes within the ontologies should be set up. The ontology can be switched to a new version until the possible effects on the application are tested thoroughly, *viz*, additional cyclic refinement are performed and evaluation phases are worked through.

2.2.3 DILIGENT

While the above two methodologies focused their effort on providing precise guidelines for an ontology development process in a tightly controlled environment, the possible developing iterations between construction/modification and the use of the ontologies are outside of their consideration. Other issues, such as *Decentralization*, which occurs quite often when the stakeholders of an ontology in many real projects are distributed and can not necessarily easily meet often, as well as *Partial Autonomy*, which is a requirement for personalizing a part of the ontology for local use, were not addressed.

In light of these issues, the DILIGENT [73] methodology extends the OTK methodology by specifying five stages to refine the ontology in response to the initiation. By providing the possibility of local adaptation, feedbacks and modifications will be gathered and analyzed by a board of ontology stakeholders, which is composed of domain experts, ontology engineers, and users. The important task for the board members is to decide which adaptations should be put into the shared ontology so as to generate a new version of the ontology. In the final stage, the new ontology will be distributed to the local sides and the updating actions will be performed. With the aim of making the ontology incrementally more mature, this process will be performed in a cyclic manner: when a new common ontology is available, a new round starts again. In each stage, the major roles, inputs, decisions, actions, available tools, and output information are elaborated. Fig. 2.4 shows the life cycle of the methodology.

Local Adaptation. With a general comprehension of the ontologies and the underlying formal representations, the users at the client side study the common shared ontology first and decide which changes need to be performed on such an ontology for a personalized application use. After the execution of several conceptualization actions, a locally changed ontology reflecting the user's needs in a better way will be generated and will be stored locally. The users must document the reasons for these decisions.

Analysis. Based on the changes proposed by the *Local Adaptation* stage, the board members will determine the changes to be introduced into the new shared ontology at the conceptual level. Several metrics will support this process of decision, such as 1. the number of users who introduced a change in proportion to all users who made changes; 2.the number of queries including certain concepts; 3. The number of concepts adoptd by the users from previous rounds. The result of this stage is a list of major changes to be introduced by agreement of the participants involved.

Revision. Taking the list of changes given by the previous stage as the major reference, the ontology board engineers can judge them more exactly from an ontological perspective at a formalization level. During this phase, attention should be paid to the potential change in accuracy formulated by the users. They also need to introduce the potentially useful concepts/relations into the new common shared ontology which are not explicitly involved in the list. When formal decisions are made, a new common shared ontology will be generated, which includes all intended changes identified during the analysis phase. The evaluation of the decisions is performed by comparing the changes on the conceptual level with the final formal decisions.

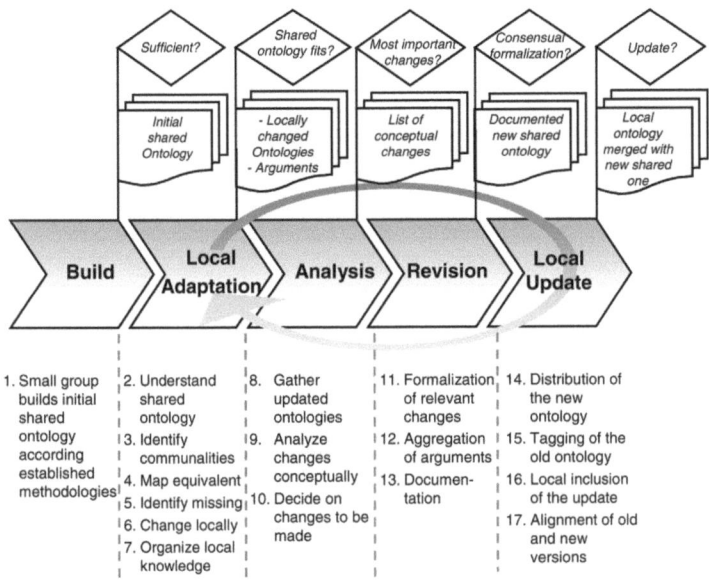

Figure 2.4: The Life Cycle of DILIGENT, Process Stages, Actions and Structures [73]

Local Update. After the new common ontology is revised and distributed, the local users decide on which changes are needed in their local ontology, depending on the differences between their own and the new shared conceptualization. In this process, the local conceptualization will not be entirely substituted by the new one.

2.2.4 A Model of Ontology Maturing

The above mentioned methodologies concentrate on defining guidelines for ontology building from scratch. A number of specific roles, such as domain experts, knowledge engineers, ontology developers, and users, are defined. At the same time, these methodologies intend to give a clear definition of the tasks for each role and their activities in any stage during the ontology development phase. With the increasing use of ontologies in many disciplines, e.g., semantic web and knowledge management, however, the requirements that end users, who do not have high level

18

competence in ontology developing, or even do not have any knowledge about ontology, are increased and should be involved in the life cycle of ontology development. Such requirements are based on several facts: a) the development of heavy-weight ontology, which contain exact logical expression of certain domain knowledge, is a time consuming work and needs specialists both in domain knowledge and ontology engineering; b) applications, which are based on these heavy-weight ontologies, face the challenge of rapid development of emerging new knowledge and change of legacy knowledge; c) ontology development is not a short-term task, it needs time to be refined and shaped.

A model of ontology maturing is proposed in [12]. This model focuses on supporting end-users in giving their knowledge to increase the maturity of the existing ontologies. There are four steps in this model and Fig. 2.5 gives an overview of it.

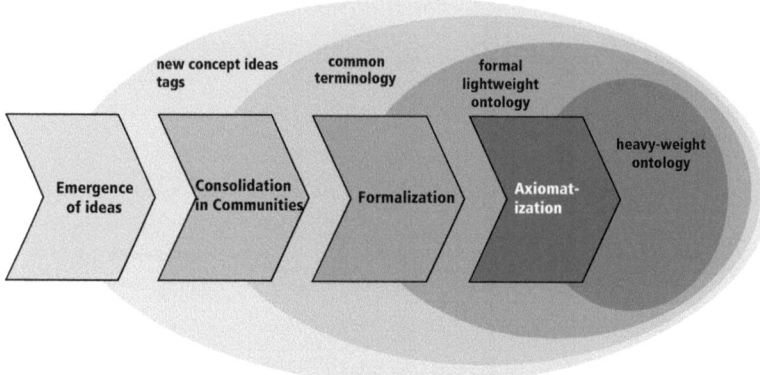

Figure 2.5: Ontology Maturing Process [12]

- **Emergence of Ideas.** In this initial transition, new informal and personal-oriented ideas are introduced, typically through tagging technique.

- **Consolidation in Communities.** A shared vocabulary in a community emerges through reuse or adaptation of tags. Concepts describing certain knowledge will be created by discovering the similarities and differences of tags through comparing the currently envisioned tags with previously used or assigned ones.

- **Formalization.** In this step, the concepts will be organized into relations, both taxonomical (hierarchical) and ad hoc relations. A lightweight ontology based primarily on subconcept relations will be generated as a result of this step.

- **Axiomatization.** More background knowledge of the concepts will be embedded into the definition to capture domain semantics. Specialists with high level competence in logical formalism will be employed in this step.

The model proposers apply primarily tagging techniques to support their maturing procedure, since only the easiest techniques can be understood by most end users, who have little or no knowledge about semantics. A tool supporting this model will be discussed in a later section.

2.3 Tool Supported Collaborative Ontology Development

While ontology engineering offers guidelines for ontology development, the tools for ontology development support the stakeholders in all stages of the ontology life cycle. Ontology editors enable implementing ontology into concrete ontology languages, such as RDF(S), DAML+OIL, and OWL. Some editors [53, 6] are standard desktop applications and provide users with a simple GUI based interface. Because ontology development is not a task for one person, several users will be included in almost every step of the entire life cycle. Collaboration support is demanding and editors such as [76, 68] try to offer support in cooperation activities. They are usually based on a server to support a shared ontology. The client side application connects to the central server and takes responsibility for controlling the edit actions performed by the developers. These tools focus on supporting developers' creating ontologies during the implementation phase, as a result, there are some platforms or environments, such as [23, 70, 82, 17, 11], aimed at offering help through the entire development stages. Most of them are based on certain ontology engineering methodologies and include a tool suite to support user activities and developing documents in each development stage. The scales of these platforms or environments are much larger, together with more complicated application than those desktop-based ones. The advantage is obvious, since they support each ontology engineering step in a controlled environment and thus lead to better supervision in the process of the development.

The dominant traditional view in ontology engineering is that the ontology development process is a time-consuming and laborious task done by highly qualified knowledge engineers with the assistance of domain specialists. However, with the appearance of Web 2.0 techniques and the accompanying new thinking on social networks, more and more less-trained or plain-knowledge users have been empowered to maintain and evaluate ontologies or even introduce new concepts into the current ontologies. Techniques used in tagging and Wikis, for example, that are nowadays familiar for many users can effectively be used for refining and maturing ontologies, which are initially created by highly trained knowledge experts. [2, 86, 34] are good examples and their results are the so-called "light-weight" ontologies, which are conceptualization or taxonomies of certain domain knowledge with few logical expressions. Such "light-weight" ontologies are good reference for ontology experts to fix bugs or extend missing concepts in the current ontologies.

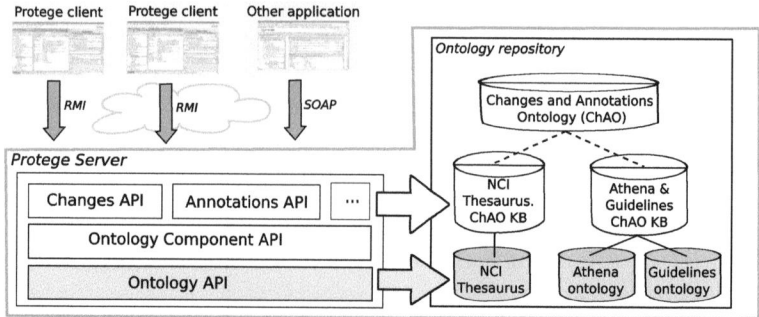

Figure 2.6: The Client–Server Architecture and the Components of Collaborative Protégé. [76]

In this section we will study several representative tools to understand the general requirements for the process of ontology development.

2.3.1 Collaborative Protégé

Protégé is a widely used open-source ontology and a knowledge-based editor [26], which can be run as a standalone application or in a client–server setting. Since the requirements of supporting collaborative actions in developing ontologies are increasing, Collaborative Protégé [76, 77] has been developed as an extension of the client–server Protégé. Assumptions on the editorial workflows for users have been minimized to enable tool customization for different workflows. Meanwhile, the key feature of such editor is that it supports **Annotations** during the ontology development process.

Fig. 2.6 presents the architecture and the main components of the Collaborative Protégé. The editor is based on a client–server structure. The Protégé server has an *Ontology Repository* that contains all the ontologies that the Protégé clients can edit in the collaborative mode. The ontology *Changes and Annotations ontology* (ChAO) [76] identifies the structure of the annotations that users would make. Each domain ontology in the repository will be associated with a ChAO ontology.

The ChAO ontology contains several modules. Fig. 2.7 depicts the overview of the ChAO ontology. The *Roles module* describes the users, roles, operations and policies that apply to a certain ontology. The *Workflows module* provides a formal language for describing workflows for collaborative ontology development. The *Ontology Components module* provides a meta-language for describing representational entities in different ontology languages. The *Annotations module* represents the different types of annotations that users make. The *Changes module* contains classes representing different types of changes that can occur in an ontology.

21

When users edit the domain ontologies in the client Protégé, each modification will be sent to the server. The server is responsible for three main tasks: (a) synchronizing the shared ontology based on the modifications made by users; (b) pushing the changes to all participants in client Protégé so that all users will notice these changes immediately; (c) creating one or more ChAO instances to represent the changes [51].

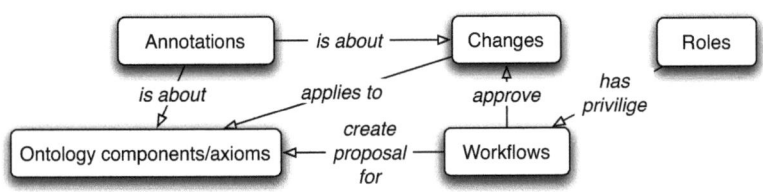

Figure 2.7: The ChAO Ontology. [51]

Several innovative graphical user interfaces have been implemented in the client Protégé. Each of the collaborative tabs supports one of the several collaborative features. In the *Annotation Tab* users could add annotations to a specific ontology resource or a specific annotation. Several annotation types have been supported, such as Comment, Question, Example, and Proposal. The ChAO identifies the structure of these annotations. In the *Discussion Thread Tab* users could conduct discussions on the ontology. For example, users could discuss that if a certain naming-space should be attached to the current ontology. The *Changes Tab* shows a chronological list of all the changes for the selected ontology component. Detailed information, such as author, data, etc., will be listed in the tab.

2.3.2 HOZO

If an ontology is very large and contains several sub-domains of knowledge, then as a choice within the development process, the ontology could be divided into several sub-ontologies. Hence, the development of the ontology as a whole can be achieved by editing and modifying its sub-ontologies individually, which are called *component ontologies*. Hozo[39, 40] has been developed based on this notion.

While these component ontologies are heavily dependent on each other, the **Relationship** and **Role** between concepts existing in different component ontologies have been investigated in order to ensure the consistency of the entire ontology. The interdependency among component ontologies is defined by the relationship of dependency between concepts defined in respective ontologies. There are [20]:

- *Super–sub* Relation (is-a relation): Two ontologies are said to be in *"super–sub relation"* if and only if there are at least two concepts in is-a relation and each of the two concepts belongs to a different ontology of the two. These ontologies then are named "upper ontology" and "lower ontology," respectively. The lower ontology depends on the upper one in terms of inheriting definitions.

22

- *Referring-to* Relation (class constraint): Once a concept in one ontology refers to a concept in another as a class constraint, then this kind of relation is called the "referring-to relation." The ontology containing the slot being constrained is called the "referring ontology" and the other, the "referred-to ontology."

While one component ontology may take multiple positions, e.g., "lower," "upper," "referring" and "referred," as a whole, multiple component ontologies and their dependencies form a graph rather than a tree.

Modifications occuring in a concept in one component ontology may influence the other concepts located in other component ontologies, to maintain the consistency of the entire ontology based on the correct management of the dependency. There are five kinds of countermeasures taken in the influenced ontology if one concept has been changed [39]:

1. To modify the influenced ontology to accept the change;

2. To leave the depending ontology influenced by the change;

3. To modify the influenced ontology to reject the change;

4. To stay compliant with the last version of the changed (depending) ontologies;

5. To break the dependency;

A study of the modifications and their possible countermeasures in other component ontologies has been performed [39]. In total, 17 types of change of the concept according to the kind of dependency, and 67 possible modification as countermeasure for the change, have been listed. Based on this modification–countermeasure map, users can choose multiple countermeasures in case a change happens in other ontologies.

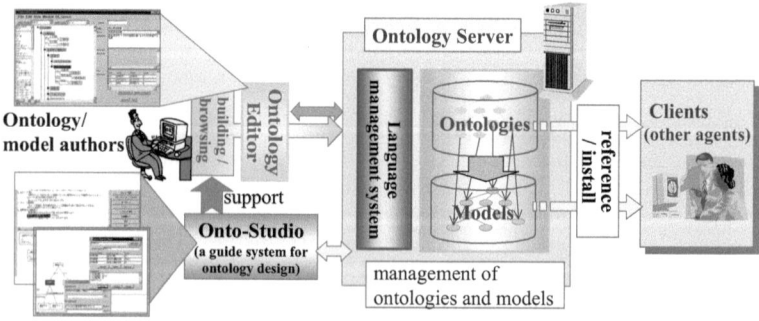

Figure 2.8: The Architecture of HOZO [39]

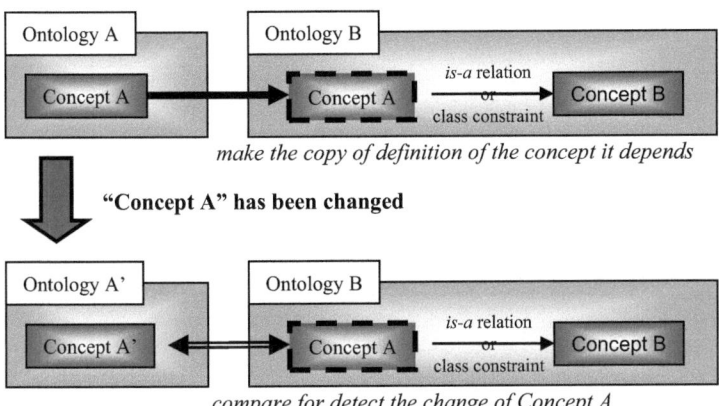

make the copy of definition of the concept it depends

"Concept A" has been changed

compare for detect the change of Concept A

Figure 2.9: Data Structure of Dependency [68]

From the consideration discussed above, HOZO has been developed to build ontologies based on fundamental ontological theories. It is composed of "Ontology Editor," "Onto-Studio" and "Ontology Server" (in Fig. 2.8). Ontology Editor provides users with a graphical interface, through which they can browse and modify ontologies. Onto-Studio is based on a method of building ontologies, named Activity-First Method (AFM) [47], and it helps users design an ontology deriving from technical documents. Ontology Server deals with the established ontologies and models.

After the user has chosen the component ontology to develop under the HOZO environment, the system will access other correlating component ontologies and compile them temporarily. A key action for the user now is to choose countermeasures listed on the Tracking Panel in order to cope with the changes made by other users. Afterwards, the user will start to edit his component ontology and eventually update his ontology on Ontology Server and publish it to others. During this modification procedure, one component ontology can be accessed by only one user, a lock mechanism will be performed to prevent any "dirty" modifications from other users.

Fig. 2.9 portrays the data structure and its application during the ontology development phase. If a concept in the current editing ontology depends on other concept (concept A) lying in extra ontology, a copy of the referred concept will be imported to the editing ontology. This copy of the concept will be used to detect and identify the change of the referring concept.

2.3.3 SOBOLEO

Ontology development is usually not a one shot activity performed by a group of experts. Instead, there is a long-term evolution towards maturity. A tool named Social Bookmarking and Lightweight Engineering of Ontologies (SOBOLEO) [86] has been implemented to support such an ontology maturing model. The goal is to develop a shared vocabulary, a shared collection of relevant web resources with a lightweight ontology editor, and an ontology-enabled social bookmarking system through working in one domain knowledge. This tool supports the first three steps in the maturing model. There are four application parts in the tool: 1) a lightweight ontology editor to support modification of the shared vocabulary; 2) a tool used to annotate the web resources; 3) a semantic search engine for the annotated web resources; 4) a taxonomy browser for navigating the taxonomy and the bookmark collection.

- **Editing.** Fig. 2.10 shows the interface of the editor. A taxonomy, including informal but not yet consolidated concepts, is displayed in a tree view on the left hand side of the interface. Detailed information of the selected concepts in the tree view will be expressed in the center part. Users could modify its relations with other concepts supported by auto completion. On the right hand side of the interface, a chat panel is employed to communicate with other users who are working together on the same ontology.

- **Annotation.** Through a pop-up window, users can modify or create a new annotation for a web resource. Necessary information, such as the title, taxonomy, as well as the comment, accompanied by the url of the web resource, will be stored in the collection.

- **Search.** The semantic based search engine allows for searching and retrieving resources within the shared bookmark collection. By entering concepts of labels all resources annotated by the concepts will be listed. Recommendations will be proposed based on the relations identified in the concepts.

- **Browsing.** By means of the browsing interface, users can navigate through the taxonomy and the associated bookmark documents. Meanwhile, the users can click through the taxonomy concepts from the root concepts.

2.3.4 Shortcomings of Current Tools

The previous section, Section 2.3, discussed several popular ontology editors which support collaborative activities. Each tool has its unique features in supporting cooperation during ontology development on the one hand, simultaneously with an absence of other features on the other hand. In this section the advantages and disadvantages of several tools will be listed and discussed.

Collaborative Protégé is a extension of client–server Protégé. The opensource editor with an architecture supporting plug-in reached a high recognition among ontology application and creation communities. The designers of the editor focused their attention on supporting asynchronous information exchange among users. Annotations are the main technique to support cooperation. For example, annotations help users raise discussions for certain concepts, users could discuss if a necessary modification should be performed within a concept following a style similar to on-line forum discussion. Discussions will be saved for future retrieval. Various types of annotation can be set upon the help of the ChAO ontology, such as discussion, voting, proposal and change. The client–server architecture offers a platform to implement immediate group awareness. However, the editor has some shortcomings in supporting versioning and social connections.

Figure 2.10: Ontology Editor Interface in SOBOLEO [86]

There does not exist an embedded version control system inside the editor. Changes performed by users will be recorded in an annotation style. Through change annotations, users could be aware of the actions of modifications and their context, such as who performed, and when, such a change, nevertheless, rolling back to a given previous state of the concept is hard. Users have to perform each counter-actions following the change history to restore the concept to its previous state, instead of a simple action of 'rollback'.

Support for the social connection of users is also absent in the editor. The *Role* module in the ChAO ontology supports identity definition of users and the defined role of a user decides his editing action in developing the ontology. However, when the number of developer increases, the organization structure of them becomes more complex. Scientists, project managers, domain experts, ontology developers, users, etc., are involved stakeholders of an ontology and they form a community in which different types of collaborative work may be performed and a large amount of information will be exchanged. A good social software is demanded and is expected to support collaboration inside the community. For example, a user could easily find out who is responsible for defining the current concept which needs to be refined, or a referenced literature can be retrieved late to check semantic meaning of an ontology class. Such activities can not be supported in Protégé.

HOZO is based on the model of roles and relationships. A large ontology can be divided into several component ontologies. The HOZO system manages the dependency relationships among different component ontologies and ensures consistency when changes happen. Component ontologies are located in a distributed environment and can be modified by multiple users. Users are required to determine the proper countermeasures if changes were performed in the component ontologies. After the users have finished editing the component ontologies, the changes will be distributed through the system and remind others to respond. The system offers each user a 'sand box' in each working space. In this private workspace, users could work on their own job without being disturbed by any of the others' activities. Concurrency control has been implemented to permit one and only one user to be working on a certain component ontology. The system, however, lacks many other collaborative supports.

The HOZO system does not support group awareness during modification. Users can only be informed that something has been changed before they start to do their modification. Changes will be distributed after editing has been saved. In the other periods of the development phase, users have no idea of what other co-workers are doing simultaneously. The granularity of concurrency control is too rough in HOZO. Even the development of relatively small component ontologies can not be done by one person. If multiple users want to do modifications on a component ontology, they have to wait and perform their changes one after the other, since only one person can edit a component ontology at the same time. This way of working wastes time and lowers efficiency. Support of synchronous and asynchronous information exchange is also missing from the system. Chatting can not be supported and annotation of a concept is also impossible.

SOBOLEO is a new tool for lightweight ontology creation and management. It is an editor based on the Web 2.0 technique. Ease of use is very important since its users do not usually possess deep understanding of ontology and semantics. Based on the ontology maturing model discussed in the previous section, a tagging tool captures the new ideas of users in the tag style. A web based editor manages the conceptualization in a lightweight model. Simple relationships of concepts can be managed in the editor with awareness of collaborative activities. The SOBOLEO system supports the first three stages of the ontology maturing model and supports management of tags and bookmarks among users on a very large scale.

The SOBOLEO system is not a full-fledged ontology editor. Complicated definitions for a concept can not be assigned. According to the ontology maturing model, the SOBOLEO system is designed to generate a lightweight ontology primarily based on subconcept relations. This lightweight ontology will then be used to help specialists build the full fledged ontology.

2.4 Comparing Ontologies

Ontology development is a process through which aims at producing a mature terminology from an initial rough draft. Different definitions of an entity will be generated from different developers at different times. As the definition of ontology is that it is a consensual agreement for a domain knowledge, different perspectives need to be unified during the development process. A number of alignment methods, including comparing and merging, are imported to help developers perform this unification process. In this section we will discuss the state of the art of ontology comparison.

The requirements of ontology comparison and mapping were first generated based on the fact that users need to find the similarity between different ontologies which are built by different groups of developers for similar but not identical purpose. A function, the so called similarity function, is normally used to calculate the similarity between two entities, providing the result in numeric format. Based on the definition given by Bisson [8], the similarity function *sim(x,y)* for two entities x and y is defined as following:

- $sim(x,y) \in [0...1]$: Similarity is *positive*.

- $sim_{x,x} = 1$: Similarity is reflexive.

- $sim_{x,y} = sim_{y,x}$: Similarity is symmetrical.

- $sim(x,y) = 1 \rightarrow x = y$: Two entities are identical.

- $simx,y = 0 \rightarrow x \neq y$: Two entities are different and have no similar features.

To decide the similarity between classes, instances, and properties, several approaches are possible, one of them [35] is that similarity functions can be classified into the *linguistic*, *structural* and *semantic* similarity . This classification orients the framework [21].

1. *Linguistic similarity* includes all language similarity calculated in the ontologies. Not only the linguistic similarity of the two words, but also the meaning of the words will be taken into account during the calculation, especially for *synonymy* and *Superordinate*. External resources will be required in this case, such as a dictionary or a thesaurus. The *Data Layer* defined in [21] is analogous to this class.

   Edit-distance [42] and *n-grams* [78] are two typical methods for this type of similarity determination.

2. *Structural similarity* considers the configuration of entities in the ontology (Ontology Layer). To evaluate the similarity of two entities, the relations between other concepts will be included. Neighboring concepts, from parent concepts to root concepts, as well as child concepts and the properties of the concept, will be involved during the calculation. The structural features which will be considered during the calculation are various. To compare two concepts, possible measures are:

   (a) the child nodes will be involved during the calculation.

   (b) the parent nodes, from the direct parent to the root nodes, may be considered.

   (c) the relative nodes, which are located in the same layer with the present node, may be involved.

   (d) the instance group of the present class.

   (e) other nodes, which are related to the present class through properties.

   The first three measures performed in the comparison are based on the consideration of *taxonomic hierarchy*. [85, 60, 43] are methods based on this consideration. The left two measures are based on the consideration of *graphic model* and [46] are typical implementations.

3. *Semantic similarity* calculates similarity based on the semantic context of the two entities. Additional information, such as a description of the concept, the interconnection between the concept and the documents, or the concept's definition in other ontologies, will be necessary for the calculation. The *Context Layer* is close to this definition.

   There are several models known from the area of *Information-Retrieval* to determine if two documents are similar. For example, [62] determines the similarity between two documents based on the terms used in the content of the documents.

Ontology evolution and versioning is one of the cases which may use ontology comparison. In this thesis we developed a system controlling version information for each entity of the ontology. The requirement in this scenario is different from other use cases. To find the similarity between two concepts from different ontologies is required in many use cases for ontology comparison, however, to find the difference between two copies of the same concept from different versions is a case in the ontology versioning scenario. In the first example we want to find whether two entities are the same given the necessary information, such as their name or their configuration. In the second example we need to tell if the entity has been changed given two snapshots taken at different times.

To determine if two snapshots of the same entity or ontology are the same is not as straightforward as it appears to be. Linguistic comparison of the triples of two copies is sufficient only if no anonymous nodes are included in the ontology graph. The existence of anonymous nodes in the ontology graph greatly increases the difficulty. [14] proposed one solution for this problem. The solution is based on alphabetical sorting of the triples. Virtual numeric IDs will be assigned to the anonymous nodes and will replace their original local names. The number of the ID is determined by the sequence of its appearance during the multiple loops. The linguistic comparison of the triples is possible when each triple contains only either an URI or a virtual ID.

Chapter 3

Requirements for Collaborative Ontology Development

The need for collaboration in ontology development is generally acknowledged. However, the study of the tools which support collaborative ontology development has only been studied in recent years and the notions of the current collaborative ontology development environments still do not support the range of functions necessary. The Collaborative Knowledge Construction (CKC) Challenge [50] revealed that even in the relatively small spectrum of these tools, from tools to organize tags to full-fledged ontology editors, there is no single tool which completely supports the range of different requirements. Not only are the maturity and the perfection of the current tools deficient, but also the understanding of the requirements of collaborative tool-supported ontology development is still not fully elaborated. Hence, in this chapter we will, based on the previous discussion of the deficiencies and shortcomings of the current tools, establish some general requirements for supporting collaboration during ontology development in an editing environment.

The three editors discussed in the previous section can be considered representative of this field. The lessons learned from them guide us to discover common requirements in supporting collaborative ontology development. Though a full list of functionalities would be very long, there are several key points to note. In this chapter we will discuss the most important requirements for ontology development in several sections based on their features.

3.1 Collaboration Requirements

As the scale of ontologies increases, a larger number developers will be included during the development, thus the need for supporting collaboration increases. Group awareness and some correlative issues, such as access management and conflict management, will be discussed in this section.

Collaborative Editing. This is the fundamental requirement demanded by collaborative ontology development. To build a single ontology, a group of developers will be working on the same copy of the ontology draft either in a shared workspace or a private workspace. All editing actions, including, e.g., modifications, discussions, voting, and reference citing, should be managed within a editing environment. Multiple clients will be involved in the process and developers can edit the ontology synchronously or asynchronously.

Group Awareness. If cooperation occurs at the same time across different places, it is useful for developers to understand what actions are made by which workers. To begin with, this helps users to develop an understanding of the group and cooperation process. Furthermore, it might avoid potential conflicts. For example, if a user realizes that another user is working on an concept related to his modification, he may inform the developer to reach an agreement of modification making. What kinds of action need to be distributed to team members is worth discussing, since not every change performed needs to be broadcast to every co-worker. Otherwise, irrelevant awarenesses may disturb personal work.

User and Access Management. The management of users and user rights is usually the fundamental requirement for collaborative work. In multiple user environments, users identify themselves by offering basic information, such as name, age, gender, etc. Changes and modifications will be related to the modifier, so that other users can easily trace the change. By comparison, the management of user rights is still deficient in the current collaborative ontology developer systems. A developer with "write" permission could change anything in the ontology. This is not acceptable in practical usage. In a real working environment, for instance, some users may have rights to change the ontology concepts in a limited knowledge domain, but *read* the whole ontology; some users may make proposals for changes but cannot change; instead, a group of users, who act as *"supervisor"* is entitled to decide which proposed changes will be performed. Those requirements need to be considered in the management of user rights. However, since concepts are usually tightly related in an ontology, which means the changes made in one concept may alter largely the meaning of other concepts, a fine-grained control of user rights is rather difficult.

Conflict Management. Conflict means that different modifications performed by different developers are applied to the same concept. The occurrence of conflicts without management leads to mis-definition. For example, a user removed a class in the ontology whereas another user tried to add a new child class for the removed class at the same time; or two users simultaneously added similar comment to a certain concept and made a redundancy. Conflicts may happen in any cooperation scenario, either same/different time or same/different places. There are commonly two mechanisms to solve this problem. One solution is to prevent the occurence of conflicts. In this case users normally need to lock the concept which is about to change and modification of the locked concept cannot be performed by other users until the lock has been released. The second solution is to merge the copies of concept definition from the different developers. In this case, there are no locks and users can make changes at any time. Private workspace is used and the system will detect conflicts based on certain detection algorithms. Usually, the modifier is responsible for merging his modification into the shared workspace manually. In some cases, the system will merge the conflicts automatically.

Workspace. Reaching consensus among developers usually implies that a commonly agreed version of work is stored in a shared work space. Many current editors that are based on the client–server architecture have such shared workspaces located on the server. The need for private workspaces depends on the user requirements. In some cases, a shared workspace is enough. However, there is an obvious disadvantage of a unique shared workspace. Many current editors use a locking mechanism to provide modification control to avoid conflicts. One possible drawback to this solution is that later users make their modifications without carefully considering the definition made by previous co-workers. Ignoring the potential knowledge conflicts is unavoidable in this environment. Conflict indicates the different understandings of a particular concept among the developers and should be brought into discussion. Offering a private workspace for each developer brings a benefit. The private workspace is a "*sand box*" in which personal opinions and thinking will be conserved. Multiple facets of knowledge can be provided and consensus reaching activities, e.g., discussion and voting, will be more efficient based on these facets. The private workspace is particularly suitable in those case, where many collisions of concept definition take place. Apart from the unique shared workspace structure, different definitions of certain knowledge can be easily stored in each user's private workspace.

Social Support. While the scope of cooperation in ontology development expands, many stake-holders may be involved in its development. Cooperation does not only contain collaborative working in a small team, where every developers knows the others. The scenario in which a very large number of users are involved in the ontology development, has to be considered. In such case, social support is demanded to help users know each other. Social networks have the capability of helping people connect more closely through a number of supports in file sharing, forum, news broadcasting, etc. Its usefulness has been recognized by research communities in the ontology development field. Some systems [19, 75] support discussions, argumentation, and voting based on wikis, which provides a natural forum for discussions, and the provenance information for suggested changes is simple to archive. Through the help of Web 2.0 techniques, the developers could build online communities for ontology development. In these online communities developers could discuss interesting domain knowledge, share relative files, argue some key issues, present alternative implementations, and vote to decide whether modifications should be performed.

Supporting Distributed, Heterogeneous Groups. Offshore software development has become increasingly popular because it can contribute to reducing the cost of a development project and can compensate a lack of resources. Different development teams located in different countries will be involved in working together on a project. When the scale of ontologies becomes so large that they are likely to be implemented by different people from different countries, heterogeneity is a problem that people may need to face. Though the knowledge representation language is possibly unique for an ontology project, developing tools to implement the ontology in such a language, for example OWL or RDF(s), may be various.

3.2 Administrative Requirements

As the ontologies become more complicated, larger development teams and more complex, longer processes will be involved. To achieve a successful final result, some administrative supports are demanded to help in controlling the development process. We discuss two fundamental requirements in this section.

Change Management. New information and knowledge will be appended to legacy ontology and errors will be removed. In a collaborative environment, achieving a consensual result includes many activities, such as brain storming, voting, annotation, etc. Meanwhile, discussions are valuable, like what is the motivation to perform such a change? Are there any other alternative possibilities to that change? What will be the possible consequences for related concepts? In addition, the development environment can serve as a kine of design rational that stores the agreement for design decision. It is easier for developers to understand the change-history of an ontology resource, such as a class or a property, with help of this documented information, even after several months, since the last modification might have been performed by a developer who is not working on the team any more.

Version Control. Performing modifications needs the support of a version control system. Reversion provides a safe and traceable environment, in which the provenance of information will be preserved. Version control systems are widely used in different environments, such as software development environments. The integration of a version control system into an ontology editor is important. Different ontology versions, as well as important modification meta-data, e.g., the name of the modifier and the time of the change, will be stored and traceable for future retrieving. There are some systems supporting revision based on SVN or CVS, in which different versions of the entire ontology have been controlled. During the development phase, a fine-grained revision system is required. Not only the entire ontology, but also each ontology resource should be traceable. The modification history offered by such revision systems is more intuitive than a list of change logs. A good integration of a revision system into an editor will give users the feeling of a safer environment and stimulate them to perform more changes which they might otherwise not make due to uncertainty of their correctness.

To build a system supporting all the above mentioned requirements is difficult. In this thesis we aim at supporting those requirements by designing and implementing two prototype systems, which serve for validation different aspects of collaborative support. The first system focuses on supporting group-awareness, lock-controlling, change management, and social supporting. In this system, ontology developers are working together in a more synchronous environment—usually in the same intranet with similar working hours. The second system explores the possibilities of supporting collaborative working in a more asynchronous and distributed environment. It provides private workspace for each developer and a shared repository, which will be used to maintain consensus and manage different versions of concept definition.

Chapter 4

Collaborative Ontology Development—the Ontoverse Use Case

The Semantic Web and the Social Web are two important trends emerging in the World Wide Web. The first one aims at information integration [1, 13, 18], whereas the second one tries to increase the capability of user communities to, e.g., produce different types of content, build relations between users, benefit communication between friends, etc. [55, 29]. Economists as well as scientific communities have started to discuss how to merge these two approaches.

To support the above mentioned techniques, the Ontoverse research project [58, 57, 45] developed a platform to support multiple users working together to create robust ontologies within scientific communities, especially in life-science communities. A WIKI based web portal has been implemented which supports setting up virtual communities; a Java-Swing based ontology editor is introduced to supporting collaborative ontology development. In this chapter we will briefly give an overview of the Ontoverse project and discuss some of its important components.

4.1 Overview of the Ontoverse Project

Ontologies will be generated through a group of people writing domain knowledge in a formal, consensual and structural format. In this process there are two kinds of resources in need of management [58]. On the one hand, this group of people should be interconnected closely so that they can easily exchange their opinions, ideas, attitudes and advice; on the other hand, the source of knowledge, e.g., journal articles and papers, as well as information generated during the development, e.g., discussions for certain concepts, must be obtained, stored, and managed so as to establish good references for the ontologies. The Ontoverse platform provides tools for designing ontologies in annotating and interlinking knowledge sources and additionally assists people to build up social (scientific) networks.

4.2 User Communities

To construct a domain ontology, both ontology engineers or information architects and domain experts are needed to formalize precise representations [58]. Therefor the knowledge and competence of these users will usually be very different. For instance, the usage of ontology languages, such as OWL and RDF(S), requires specific technical skills and expertise, and the process of ontology engineering requires experiences with knowledge representation methods. On the other hand, domain ontologies usually focus on very specialized domains of interest and thus demand very detailed expert knowledge in these domains.

The ideal community for building domain ontologies would therefore comprise both domain experts (DE) and ontology designers (OD). The system should support their collaboration and condense their knowledge to build well-formed and consistent ontologies. Even though many domain experts may be not familiar with knowledge representation techniques in this community, they might contribute valuable data if provided with easy to use systems for knowledge input and additional help from ontology designers.

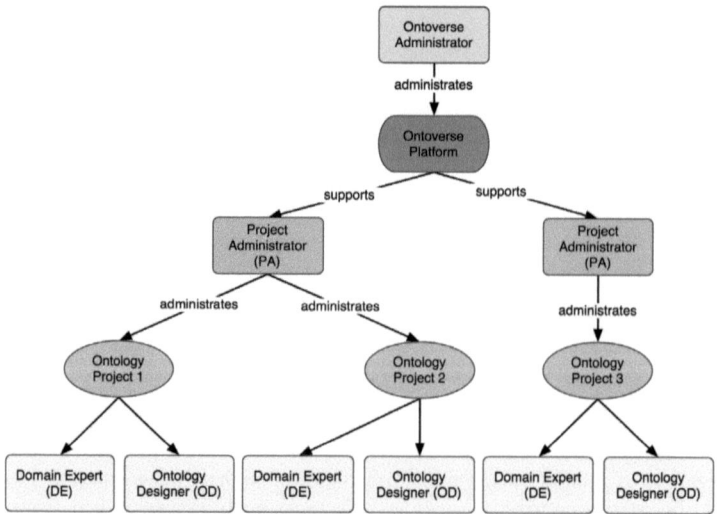

Figure 4.1: User Roles Addressing in the Ontoverse Project [58]

Hence the Ontoverse platform distinguishes the roles of OD and DE, as the interfaces and modification rights are different for each of them. For instance, once the user logins to the platform as a DE, the system provide him with a less complex user interface that does not include options for editing the actual ontological data—although they might be viewed and commented on. Principally, every user will be able to choose whether to act in the role of an OD and/or a DE. Besides these two roles, there is the special role of project administrator (PA), who is responsible for final decisions and for coordinating discussions of the other project members. Fig. 4.1 shows the structure of user communities within the Ontoverse platform.

4.3   Ontology Life Cycle within the Platform

The very first step to work within the platform can be described as follows [58]: A scientist who needs an ontology for a specific domain may first check existing ontologies for this domain. If one of them fits her needs, she can join the project as OD and/or DE and actively contribute to the project or passively view and use the data. If none of the existing projects is suitable, she initiates her own ontology project from scratch, becoming its PA automatically.

One major focus of the Ontoverse platform is the support of all phases in the ontology life cycle process as illustrated in Fig. 4.2. Because during collaborative ontology development, other ontology engineering methodologies, the goals of the ontology, the scope of interest in domain knowledge as well as in the target group should use it in a clearly defined way in the first step, this information will be stored in an ontology requirement specification document (ORSD), modified from [71]), where fundamental determinations can be precisely documented. The PA may prohibit further editing and changing of the ORSD if she thinks that a usable state has been reached.

Furthermore, thematic discussions and the collection of semistructured data in terms of knowledge acquisition are important steps within the early ontology development process. This non-formalized knowledge, such as planning and conceptualization, is particularly necessary to support the DEs in the Ontoverse platform. The platform thus provides a wiki where DEs can enter their domain knowledge in different ways. DEs may enter textual concepts in the form of glossaries, single concepts with explanations and definitions, unstructured collections of concepts, or other notes and references to external sources. DEs may upload documents as well. Discussions, modifications and changes can be traced and assigned to their authors within the wiki. This proto-ontological data builds a solid knowledge base for the ontology development performed by the ODs.

The ODs will then build up ontologies via another channel: the web-based, multi-user ontology editor. This high-level support of formal ontology engineering actually constitutes a major part of the Ontoverse project and will be elaborated in Section 5.

40

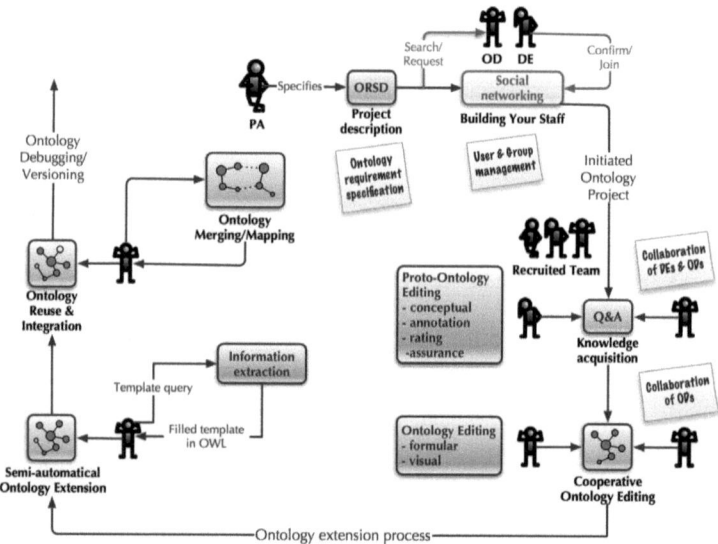

Figure 4.2: The Life Cycle of the Ontoverse Platform [58]

4.4 Important Project Results

The basic idea for the Ontoverse project was to provide a place where users are free to create, edit and modify ontologies and to do this as a member of a community of users with the same interests. A formal ontology editor is endowed with basic wiki features. These features include easy to handle, web-based, multi-user support, change tracking and notifications, undoing changes, options for discussing the current state, etc. Formal ontology engineering functionalities, social networking aspects, social and semantic tagging and information extraction mechanisms are also supported in the Ontoverse project.

Major innovations are, in brief, as follows [58]:

1. **Open Collaboration.** The project brings domain experts and ontology designers together to build the ontology in good quality based on their different abilities. Different expertise of user groups are taken into account and different access rights and division of work can be envisioned.

2. **Full Life Cycle Supporting.** The project supports all the ontology development life cycle, particularly the planning and conceptualization phase in ontology engineering. The project facilitates the organization of the proto-ontological, which is a piece of information that has not been brought into a formal ontology, e.g., the ontology requirement specification, rating and anno-

41

tation of concepts by means of the establishment of a proto-ontological area, in which domain experts can offer their knowledge and discuss it with other experts.

3. **Embedded Formal Editor.** A collaborative, web-based, formal ontology editor was developed to facilitate data storing and modification. Interactive ontology visualizations are included, together with options for integrative ontology mapping and merging. [87]

4. **Integration of Informal Wiki Based Forum and Formal Editor.** During the development process, much information, such as discussions for choosing the proper name for a concept, will be generated and stored in the Wiki based forum. Such informal information can be used as a reference to ontology resources and can, for example, help ontology developers better understand the definition of the concept. Through the user interface of the formal editor, developers could easily enter into the related forum regarding the current editing of the ontology resource.

5. **Information Extraction.** Publications are one kind of knowledge source from which to gather information about a domain. Within the Ontoverse project, a publication database is employed as the knowledge source for an information extraction application. Relevant concepts, relations and instances will be identified and later incorporated into the ontologies. In return, the newly developed ontologies themselves will help to retrieve relevant documents from the database.

6. **Index/Tagging Supporting.** Different types of content indexing were included:

   (a) Original keywords assigned to the documents were recorded, such as by authors or in professional indexing processes.

   (b) Ontology terms from any ontology kept in the project can be added to publications automatically.

   (c) Registered users can tag publications with their own keywords.

Chapter 5

An Ontology Editor with Novel Cooperation and Visualization Functions

The Ontoverse editor, a collaboration supporting formal ontology editor, is one of the key components in the Ontoverse platform. It enables ontology developers to work interactively during the development life cycle. Since the editor is closely inter-connected with the wiki platform, also non-technic domain experts can use it to view detailed ontology definitions for the various domain concepts. In this section we will discuss its architecture and innovative features.

5.1 Challenges in Developing the Editor

The editor focuses on providing an environment in which multiple users are working together to create a consistent ontology which may contain hundreds or thousands of concepts. Some important issues demand consideration in designing such system. They are:

Resolving Access Conflicts. In the collaborative ontology development environment, multiple developers may start working on the same concept at the same time. In such a case, it is possible that developers lose the outcome of their work because it is overwritten by other developers. This is an access conflict during the modification process. Principally there are two conflict resolution mechanisms adopted in multi-user environments. The first approach aims at avoiding the occurring of conflicts by means of locking. Only one user has the right to access the resource and make modifications to it. Those who want to perform modifications of the same resource will have to wait until the current one finishes working so that the access right can be handed over. An alternative approach is to merge the conflicted copies afterward. In this approach users make modifications on their own copy of the ontology. Then they need to manually merge their copies with the shared standard ones when conflicts occur. The selection of such two mechanisms depends on a requirement analysis.

Elaborated Visualization Techniques. The scales of domain ontologies are various. The number of ontology resources varies from scores of dozens to hundreds of thousands in order to present complex ontologies and concept relations in human readable form. Ideally the system can detect the field of interest of users and gives them a personalized view of the content, e.g., only the most important relations and concepts related to the current modifying concepts to be displayed to the users.

Synchronous Communication Support. While the Ontoverse wiki platform focuses on supporting asynchronous communication among users, such as forum, annotation, tagging and voting, the editor needs to provide users with a synchronous environment where users can be closely inter-connected. Events of creation, modification and deletion of ontology resources are broadcast immediately so that groupware interfaces of What-you-see-is-what-I-see (WYSIWIS) are realized.

5.2   Scenario: Collaborative Ontology Development in the Ontoverse Editor

The following description identifies a typical use case in operating the collaborative ontology editor. We employ a small sample animal ontology and define several concepts for it. In order to keep it simple, a number of information items of the ontology are omitted, such as annotations and file header. This demo ontology will be reused in a scenario in a later section, where the creation of an ontology is under the control of an ontology versioning system.

Tim and Lang are both ontology designers for the ontology project "Creatures." After they login onto the Ontoverse platform, they will join the collaborative creation of the ontology by opening the web-based formal ontology editor. Then they will be aware of the participation of other users through the *Chat* panel displayed in the editor.

Tim creates a new ontology class of *"vo:Predator"* on his client application. The event of the modification will be delivered to all involved users. Lang will notice that a new class named "vo:Predator" is displayed on his class hierarchical view, and an icon will be connected to this class indicating the collaborative modification performed. When Lang starts to change the meaning of the class "vo:Felid" by adding a new comment for this class, the class will be automatically locked by the system so that other users have no write rights to access the resource. A lock icon indicates the current state of the right limits.

A list of historical change actions helps users track the change information. In this list Lang will notice that Tim has changed the name of "vo:Felid" two days ago. On disagreeing with this modification, Lang sends Tim a "notification" and starts to state his opinion through the Chat component. With the help of this notification, Tim could easily see the topic that Lang intends to discuss.

5.3 The Backend of the Editor

A client–server based architecture is used to support event publication among several clients. The main objective of this is to be as flexible as possible to integrate several features in a loosely coupled way into one main component, which provides the basic functionality of ontology management. The backend functionality of the editor was developed by one of the research partners of the project (the COLLIDE group at the University of Duisburg-Essen). Its main concepts and architecture are described in [45].

The basic architectural idea lies in adopting a so-called blackboard system [22]. This loosely coupled system has a remarkable advantage: on the one hand it is quite flexible and easy to extend (just write another agent), on the other hand it is quite robust concerning the failure of single components.

SQLSpaces [84], which is an implementation of a type of blackboard system called **TupleSpaces** and holds different spaces on the server, was chosen to build the backend. It was developed by the Collide Research Group at the University of Duisburg-Essen with plentiful advantages over other well-known implementations, such as enhanced persistence (due to the underlying relational database, which may be MySQL, HSQLDB or PostgreSQL), versioning support and multi-language support.

An agent system called **SWAT** (Semantic Web Application Toolkit) [45] was developed on the SQLSpaces. The specific division into spaces of SWAT is shown in Fig. 5.1. There are three spaces located on the server. The ontology space (a space per ontology project) stores the ontological data in form of RDF triples. The session space contains all process-related data, such as login/logout events, creation/modification/deletion events, lock events, etc. The command space acts as a coordination channel for all participating agents.

Several agents have already been implemented. The *hotspot* agent detects the actions performed on certain concepts and calculates the value of the interest. The higher this value is, the larger the frequency of change actions. The *IO* agent is responsible for importing and exporting ontologies to and from OWL/XML files. The *operator* manages all running agents. Unique IDs will be assigned to each running agent for identification. And the *Executor* is an agent that encapsulates the knowledge of how to start the agents.

The so-called *SWAT Client* encapsulates all features of SWAT in an easily accessible Java class. One of its main tasks is to translate the RDF triples into easily manageable OWL-related Java objects. Interfaces and classes are offered to hide the detailed implementation of agents and spaces from the front-end system.

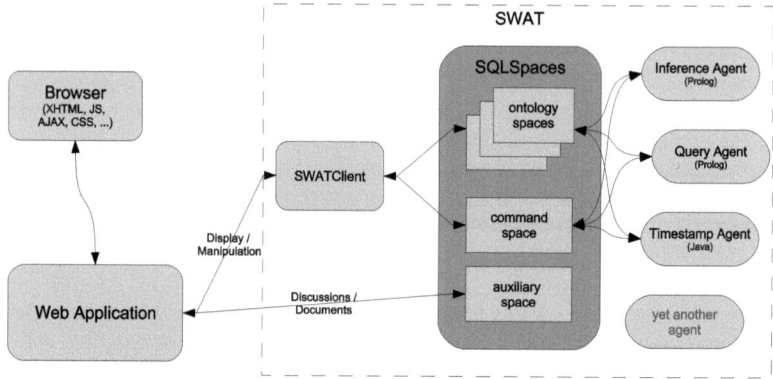

Figure 5.1: The Architecture of the SWAT Platform [45]

5.4 New Visualization Components for Ontology Editing

Based on the SWAT client, a Java-based formal ontology editor was developed in this thesis. It supports collaborative working among several users and interconnects closely with the wiki platform in the Ontoverse environment. Fig. 5.2 indicates the visualization of the editor.

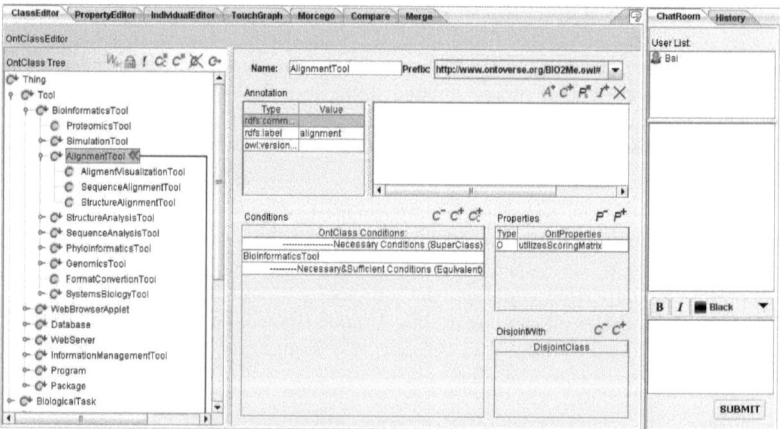

Figure 5.2: The Visualization of the Ontoverse Editor

Fig. 5.2 depicts the interface of the editor. The editor GUI is composed of two parts. The left side is the editor part, where several sub-editors have been integrated. A class editor, a property editor, and an individual editor offer ontology developers the ability to manipulate ontologies. There are two ontology visualization functionalities: TouchGraph and Morcego. These graphs offer users a graphical view of the ontologies. An interactive tool called iMerge for comparing and merging ontologies that has been developed in a related thesis [35] is also embedded in the system, so that users can compare and merge two different ontologies. The right side is the functionality part, consisting of a chat room and an ontology resource history viewer. Through this chat room users can know with whom they are working and in addition, each user can chat with the others. The history viewer gives an overview of the modification process. By selection alongside the hierarchical tree viewer, the modification history records of each ontology resource can be presented.

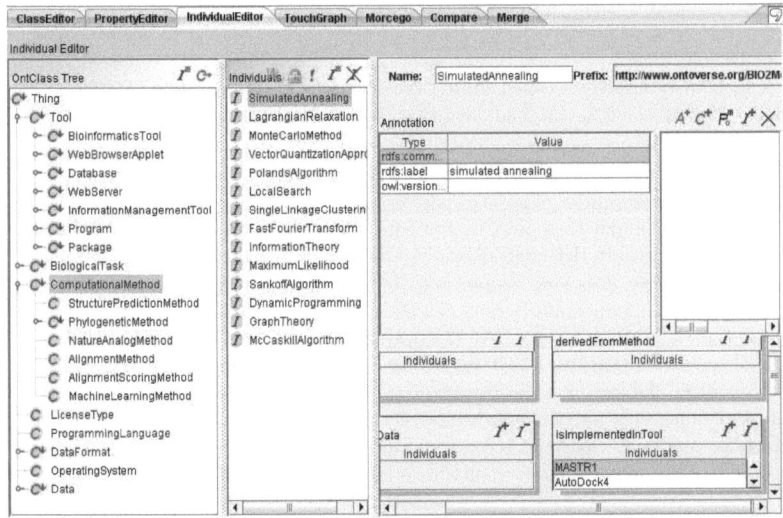

Figure 5.3: Editing Individuals

We will discuss the ontology resource editors in more detail. First of all, there is a class editor, a property editor, and an individual editor. Every editor uses a similar layout. On the left side there is a hierarchical tree viewer, which indicates the hierarchical taxonomy structure of the ontology resources. The class editor shows the ontology class hierarchical structure whereas the property editor shows the ontology property. In the individual editor, a tree viewer visualises the ontology class and a list viewer presents the current ontology class individually in accordance with the user's own selection in the tree. This is shown in Fig. 5.3. Beside the hierarchical tree viewer, on the right side there is an edit panel. The edit panel offers users the possibility to modify ontology resources. For example, in the edit panel users could add, remove and edit the annotations of each ontology resource. Besides, an ontology class users could add and remove its super classes, equivalent classes and disjoint classes in the editor panel.

This editor supports several key collaborative features and will be further discussed in the following paragraph.

5.4.1   Visualization of Large Class Hierarchies (SmartTree)

The interface of the ontology resource editors is composed of two main parts. A tree component was employed on the very left side of the editor. It shows the ontology hierarchical structure. Since an ontology may contain a large number of resources, a plain Java tree component has difficulty presenting this amount of contents. It is therefore hard for users to find the resources that they are currently interested in. Moreover, relative resources, e.g., those ontology classes equivalent to the current one, are also hard to indicate on the tree. To solve this dilemma, we developed an extended tree component called **SmartTree**, an extended tree component based on the user interface of the original Java tree object.

This tree highlights important tree nodes while maintaining the original tree structure. Functionalities of *shrink* and *spread* were developed. They can help users filter those tree nodes that users do not care about currently. The relevance of the nodes can be flexibly determined by the application. In the editing environment, users can set tree nodes as "important" by manually typing "ctrl+E." Once the nodes are set to "important," users can shrink the tree by clicking a button beside the root node or a parent node. In this way, a shrunk tree is formed that indicates only those nodes that are either important or have important children. All other nodes will be hidden. Yet, users can expand the shrunk tree at any time, either the whole one, or a particular sub-tree. By providing this focus-and-context visualization, users can easily perceive any interesting resources while maintaining an overview of the complete class structure, which may be very large.

In addition to the "parent–children" relationship, the tree supports a further visualization feature of indicating relationships. It is useful for illustrating relations among ontology resources. For example, the definition that a database could store data format information will be defined as "vo:Database vo:offersData vo:Data." This definition will not be indicated on the tree component though it is quite important for users to get such awareness. On the SmartTree interface, such relations will be illustrated by a line with an arrow head, as shown in Fig. 5.4. The arrow points from the subject to the object of the relation. Because getting such information needs a time-consuming calculation, the indication of such relation needs manual triggering, and only one concept could show its relations on the tree interface at once. Showing relations for several source and target concepts simultaneously is usually not comprehensible for the user.

49

The figure5.4 is a screenshot illustrating how *SmartTree* supports those features. The class "Program" has several properties pointing to some other classes. These ontology properties are expressed as arrows. The property's domain class is in the source of the arrows and the range classes are their targets. All related classes are marked as important nodes and are painted in a different color and font style. Once users click on the icon put on the right side of "Program" (shrink), any other nodes which have no relation with "Program" will be replaced by a "..." node and will disappear from the tree component, thus only the important nodes are left and a much clearer overview of them is displayed. Meanwhile, users can click either "..." node or its parent node's right arrow icon to see these replaced nodes again (spread).

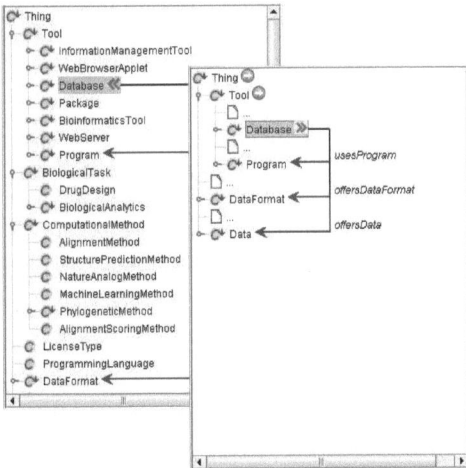

Figure 5.4: The Visualization of a SmartTree Component. Only important nodes and their relations have been displayed on the interface.

5.4.2 Group Awareness

What You See Is What I See (WYSIWIS) is a term for a groupware interface that guarantees all users will view the same content at the interface. It may be the easiest way for users to coordinate their actions during collaborative working. The editor supports this feature and users can be informed of each other's working status.

Group awareness is implemented through the event-dispatching mechanism. Once a modification is performed by a user, an event will be generated and be dispatched to all registered clients. For example, if a user creates a new ontology class, a class creation event will be generated and sent to all clients. Once a client editor receives such an event, it will get the new class from the server and build it onto the tree taxonomy. An icon will be displayed beside this new concept pointing out that this concept is created by someone else. The editor will perform such modification on the tree taxonomy only when these nodes should be displayed for users. For example, a new class in a domain knowledge creates in a user's editor, clarifying the concept of "cat" is created under the parent concept of "mammal." Other users, who are working currently on other domain knowledge, e.g., "plant," do not expand the class taxonomy of "mammal" and will not notice such a new class immediately, since it is not necessary for them to see this change. However, they will realize that the concept is newly created by other users when they expand the class taxonomy of "mammal" by clicking the icon beside the concept.

Detailed information, such as who has made this modification and when he has done it, will be only displayed in a message box when users hover the mouse over the icon. The collaborative icon can be removed once the user clicks the concept to see detailed information or wants to alter it.

In the current implementation all logged users will receive every editing awareness from other users. No filters can be defined to reduce the number of events one user may got. It raises unnecessary overload and in some cases frequent notification of awareness may be bothersome. In chapter 8 we discuss a possible solution for providing more meaningful notification to users. In this case users are aware of only those events which they really need to be care of.

5.4.3 Discussion Triggers and Chat

While group awareness provides users an "after-event" mechanism to inform them of the working statuses of each other, the editor also supports a "before-event" mechanism for users to get consensual agreement on modification before they make changes on a certain concept. This feature is called "**Discussion Triggers** and is usually applied when the user want to trigger a discussion with other developers.

One of the developer can trigger the function by clicking the button of "Discussion Trigger". A nudge event will be pushed to all clients in the same session. Once the editor receives such a nudge event, it will analyze which concept the event contains and find out the corresponding node position on the tree component. An icon showing as a blinking exclamation mark will be attached to this node on the tree. If the node is not displayed, e.g., the parent node without previous expansion, the tree will expand all its parent nodes to guarantee that the node will be noticeable by users. This icon will be removed if users click on the concept to see detailed information.

Following the notification event, users can use an embedded chat room to exchange their opinions about a change. A list of all contactable users offers a clear overview of who is working together. Under the list a shared discussion board displays all discussion messages exchanged among users. Users can input their messages into the bottommost message box and send it to all other users. They could drag and drop an ontology resource from a tree component and send a "hyper-link" message to the others by directly clicking on this message to view the resource information. Different font styles and colors may also be selected. The last sender will be marked with an icon beside his portrait in the user list.

5.4.4 Locking Mechanism

We included a locking mechanism as a solution for conflict management in our multi-user environment. The locking mechanism identifies the consequences of alterations and each time only one user has the right to perform a change, which effectively prevents the generation of conflicts. Before users edit an ontology resource, a lock will be set on the resource and only the lock holder has right to change the resource. The lock will be released after the modification is finished. However, one shortcoming of using a locking mechanism is that it may lead to low efficiency especially if many users want to change the same concept at almost the same time. This problem will be partly solved if the actions of locking and unlocking do not need manual triggering.

Two different methods for setting and removing locks in the editor were developed. The first method is called "automatic setting." In this situation, users do not need to explicitly set or release the lock from concepts. When a user starts to change an ontology resource, such as adding a new comment for an ontology class, a lock will be automatically appended to that resource after he triggers the corresponding function button, a comment-adding button in this case. As a consequence of such lock setting on the ontology resource, all function buttons in other users interface will be disabled, so that other users can not perform any change actions on this resource. Meanwhile, an icon will be attached to that resource on the tree component indicating that the resource is under modification. Users will understand who is working on the resource now by hovering the mouse on the icon. Once the modifier switches to another concept, the editor will assume that he has finished his modification and will release the lock from the current resource. In this process, the modifier does not notice the actions of lock setting and removing and this will largely speedup the modification process.

Though the automatic method fits most editing cases, it does not control the access rights of relative ontology resources. For example, modifying an ontology class potentially changes the definition of all classes which are defined as equivalent with it. In this circumstance users may not expect someone else to change the definitions of these equivalent classes and they must be locked at the same time. The editor thus offers another method to support this requirement. In performing lock management in this way, users need to manually set and release the locks before they start to modify. Multiple concepts will be locked following the user's wish. Similar to automatic setting, function buttons for the locked resource will be disabled when other users want to modify them. The switching action performed in the tree component will not release the locks. Users need to explicitly release the locks by clicking the locking function button.

5.4.5 History Tracing

Information about the evolution of an ontology containing data such as "who created this class and when has it been modified", or the reasons that lead to previous changes, can be important for both developers and users. By analyzing the change reports, they can better comprehend a concept and get a clear understanding of how it developed over time.

In the editor, a history tracing function panel is located beside the chat room on the right-hand side of the editor. In this panel a list of change actions is displayed. From this list users can easily find out who has made what kind of modification for the current ontology resource and when.

5.4.6 Interaction with the Wiki

The Ontoverse platform includes a wiki platform which supports domain experts, who are familiar with articulating their knowledge and opinions in proto-ontological format. Though they usually do not have enough experience in transforming domain knowledge into ontology and they usually do not have modification rights to change the ontology resources, it is necessary for them to be conscious of the definition of certain concepts in the ontologies.

The editor supports bi-directional access of information located on the wiki platform and the ontology editor. Once the users view the concept on the wiki platform, they can open the editor to see detailed ontological definitions by clicking a button on the web page. The wiki platform will trigger an event and send it to the editor which contains the name of the concept. The screen will be switched to the editor interface. The editor will find the corresponding ontology resource and display the relevant information on the editor's interface.

From the editor side, there is a function button to facilitate browsing wiki information on the web. Once the ontology developers click the button, the Ontoverse platform will open the wiki page for the current working ontology resource, so that developers can be aware of the proto-ontological information from it.

5.5 Some Points Learned from the Project

The Ontoverse project supports ontology developers in a platform where various documents and information related with the ontology can be preserved and traced. Multiple roles of users including ontology users, ontology developers, as well as domain experts and project managers, work in a closely interrelated environment to collaboratively develop the ontology. We have gained an understanding of a number of points about collaborative ontology development from experiences of the platform development and its later use.

The functionality of the management of literature used as references to define concepts in a development environment is required by many users. Knowledge acquisition is a typical process during ontology development where knowledge resources will be collected. In the scientific area these knowledge resources are mainly papers, technical reports, articles from journals, etc. These resources, accompanied by the knowledge in the expert's head, are the foundation for developing and building the ontologies. While the ontology is a formally structured and relatively simplified definition of knowledge, people, especially the end user, need the original sources of such knowledge in case of understanding the definition later in usage. Ontology developers also need this literature to conceptualize the knowledge, thus they demand that the literature should be managed and administered in a proper manner so that knowledge resources will be saved as a part of the entire result of the project. The functionality offered by the Ontoverse platform supports such a requirement. Papers and reports will be imported into the project to help developers get a conceptualization through manual or semi-automatica methods. Tracing of knowledge resources though the ontology resource is also possible.

A forum is a useful support for discussion and argumentation. Different understandings and perspectives of domain knowledge are usual during the development process. The procedure of getting consensual definition though discussion or argumentation helps us get a precise conceptualization. While tag is commonly used as the method to support asynchronous communication, such as Collaborative Protégé, an on-line forum supports a better communication channel for developers. More text can be written within the forum and multimedia resources can be imported into it.

The separation of domain experts and ontology developers simplifies the administration of ontology development and avoids the problem where too many developers have the right to change the ontology. However, administrative authority of the Ontoverse platform stays remains at a relatively rough level. The platform assumes that the domain experts have rights to view the ontology but developers have rights to edit the ontology. A detailed separation of editing rights is also required. For example, the ontology developer in one domain does not have the right to change the ontology part in another domain. Or the ontology developer can only change the definition of the ontology resource and can not delete or create the ontology resource.

Group-awareness supports ontology developers in working closely together. An appropriate level of awareness of activities performed by other users provides ontology developers with a better understanding of the evolution of the project. We also noticed the fact from later usage that the published collaborative events can not always be recognized by developers. Those activities, which are not related to the current working area of the developer, will be easily ignored. The awareness events which are distributed and visualized in the Ontoverse editor did not take the individual perspective of developers' domain into account. When the ontology developers receive too many unimportant notices, those they do not need to care about, such as modifications occurred in a domain which they do not understand, they are likely to ignore the important events that they should notice. At the end of this thesis we propose a possible solution for this problem.

The modification history can be traced in the form of a list of logs. If we take into accout the fact that reading a long list of plain text is boring, then we see tha a log is not the most intuitive way to provide users with the evolution information of an ontology resource. The relationship between the resource version and the ontology version is also important. Users usually require that they should be aware of the evolution of certain ontology resources when the entire ontology changes from the first version to the second version. They want to know which ontology resources have been changed and how they evolved, the reasons for performing such modifications are also important to be aware of. The list of logs can not support such complicated requirements and we need to find a new method.

The concerns about data loss caused by operational mistakes increases when the ontology becomes large. While the ontology data is located in a shared environment and every developer has rights to modify it, operational mistakes are practically impossible to avoid. Version control on each ontology resource is expected to solve this problem. When users make operational mistakes on a concept, they can roll back their working copy to a stable version.

Chapter 6

A Resource-Level Versioning Mechanism for Ontology Editing

While the Ontoverse editor provides functions for collaborative ontology development, there are still several key requirements which have not been fulfilled. In particular, the question of how to control different ontology versions in an appropriate manner during the development process is still open. We extended the ontoverse editor to provide a fine-grained versioning mechanism that provides version control at the level of individual resources and thus offers a novel technique for supporting the ontology development process in distributed environments. We will firstly introduce the motivation and challenges of developing such system. Theoretic foundation will be introduced before the function and GUI introduction of the system.

6.1 Motivation

Most of current ontology developing tools and environments implemented their applications with a centralized data structure in which there exists only one copy of the working ontology. A typical feature of these tools is the support of synchronous cooperation such as group-awareness and chatting. However, the ontology development communities have begun to realize the drawbacks of such structure. For example, though group-awareness informs related developers of their working status, it is still likely to annoy people that their work has been overwritten by another user without warning. Also, users sometimes prefer to create their own part of an ontology in a protected environment before he shares it to others. Another issue bothering developers is that they may miss important updates of certain concepts because either they did not pay attention to change notifications or they just left their work place for a while. Working in a synchronous, closely interconnected and data-centralized environment presents its vulnerability when users do not work in same time. We suggest that asynchronous, loosely connected and data-distributed environment have benefits compared to current tools. In such environments, users may protect their own part of work before they share it with the rest of the team. Through data synchronization users can also become aware of conflicts of concept definition while they have different understandings to a concept.

Asynchronous working is possible and users will not suffer from losing important information.

In this chapter we propose a novel approach and a system to provide these features in a distributed environment. In this approach, ontology developers can interact with independent personal workspaces so that each developer's personal perspective on the domain knowledge is fully considered. During the developing process, by means of updating, comparing, merging and committing, the different individual perspectives of the domain knowledge will be united in the shared ontology. This situation is similar to typical software development processes where programmers work on their local machines and share a public version on the server via version control systems such as SVN or CVS. While the rational synchronizing units for this process are usually ontology resources, the current systems cannot be used to support our requirement because they control version at the level of ontology files instead of controlling version at the level of ontology resources.

Current ontology development systems are deficient in managing independent personal perspectives. In addition, traceability of the development process is missing in many systems as well. These shortcomings are mainly engendered by the fact that current systems are not based on an architecture consisting of distributed personal workspaces and a central repository representing the current integrated view as well as the history of personal perspectives.

6.2   A Brief Introduction of Some Vocabularies

In this chapter we will discuss how do we implement the resource-level versioning mechanism in detail. To better understand the theory used in our implementation, we prefer to introduce some vocabularies which will be used in the later part in this chapter.

The basic element of an RDF ontology is a set of statements about resource in the form of subject-predicate-object expressions. We usually use the term "Triple" to describe such statement which is built up by subject, property and object. RDF graph is introduced to visualize RDF ontologies. In Figure 6.1 we will see an example. Subject and object are indicated as round shape, we also call them "RDF node" in the graph. Meanwhile the arrow indicates the property.

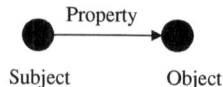

Figure 6.1: RDF graph of a Triple

The round shape may be solid which means that this node has an URI. It may also be dashed and indicates a *blank node*. A blank node does not have an URI. However, systems, which are used to manipulate the ontologies, such as *Jena*, usually assign an ID with random number to the node to ease the node manipulation.

The basic idea of our implementation is that we make two copies of an RDF unit, one on the client side and one on the server side, identical. The term *"synchronization"* will be used to explain such process. To make both units identical, we may overwrite the server side unit with the copy from the client side, or vice versa. Another possible approach is that we change both client and server units to receive a consistent copy.

6.3   Challenges in Providing Versioning Support

A workshop organized in 2006 [50] studied a fundamental question about collaborative ontology development: what are the user requirements for designing a collaborative ontology developing system? Among the requirements gathered from experts there are two requirements that are not yet fully implemented by existing solutions:

- The system should support both private and public workspaces.

- The different versions of an ontology should be adequately managed and controlled by the system.

In section 2.3 we studied several systems, most of them employ merely a shared public workspace. All developers work on the same space. Many of them focus their efforts on group awareness and concurrency control, etc. An approach that supports private and shared workspaces is HOZO[68]. HOZO splits large ontologies into several small sub-ontologies. It analyzes the dependencies of these sub-ontologies and offers a mechanism to manage them during development. The sub-ontologies can be developed on a local machine. However, if a sub-ontology is in editing mode, only one user can access it each time; a locking mechanisms prevents other users from editing.

Various aspects of ontology versioning are discussed in [36]. The authors suggest that ontology resources, such as classes, properties and instances, should have their own versioning identification so that changes can be traced. There are a few specialized ontology version control systems ,such as [83]. Some platforms also offer version control services, such as [25]. However, all these systems provide only version identifiers for a complete ontology file and cannot track versions of individual ontology resources. This makes them difficult to trace the history of a particular ontology resource.

A task in company with ontology versioning is the representation of ontology changes. Some ontology editors provide simple change logs for users. The form of these logs varies considerably. Some of them provide user context, others submit merely a sequence of changes. A framework based on PROMPTDIFF[52] visualizes changes between uncontrolled, de-centralized environments. Two different versions of an ontology are presented next to the other, highlighting the parts where changes have occurred. PromptViz [66] is a tool based on [52] which provides advanced visualizations using treemaps to help users understand the location, impact, type, and extent of changes that have occurred between versions of an ontology. One disadvantage of both tools is that they do not offer users a clear explication of the changes that happened sequentially during the entire development process.

To overcome these shortcomings of existing tools, a method is required to support incremental synchronization which makes different copies of an ontology, distributed over several locations, identical. Versioning information should be provided for the individual ontology resources so that changes can be more easily tracked and represented visually. From these requirements, a number of research questions arise that we aim to solve:

- what is an appropriate level of granularity for synchronizing ontologies between different workspaces?

- how to determine the parts of an ontology to be synchronized?

- how to compare and merge different versions of an ontology resource?

Finding an appropriate level of granularity for splitting an ontology into several small units is a prerequisite for incremental synchronization. Each time, only the changed units need to be transmitted and synchronized. Minimum Self-contained Graph (MSG) [48] provides a possible solution for this purpose. Using the MSG mechanism, an RDF graph can uniquely divided into a number of sub-graphs. According to [48] the formal definition of MSG is:

- *Definition 1.* An RDF statement involves a name if it has that name as subject or object.

- *Definition 2.* An RDF graph involves a name, if any of its statements involves that name.

- *Definition 3.* Given an RDF statement s, the Minimum Self-Contained Graph (MSG) containing that statement, written MSG(s), is the set of RDF statements comprised of the following:

  - The statement in question

  - Recursively, for all the blank nodes involved by statements included in the description so far, the MSG of all the statements involving such blank nodes;

However, it is not straightforward to use it by many current ontology editors. The smallest units defined in MSG and editors are different. Users usually take ontology resources, which can be divided into a number of MSGs according to the definition, as the smallest units in editors. Synchronization mechanism for editors thus need to synchronize changed ontology resources instead of changed MSGs.

The existence of anonymous ontology resources is extensive in many formal ontology languages, such as OWL, RDF(S). Different from named ontology resources, where URI is the identification for each resource, anonymous resources do not have a unique identification to indicate themselves. Distinguishing different copies of same anonymous resource located in different clients is therefore harder than for named resources. The problem will be amplified if we want to trace the change history of an anonymous resource. Once several anonymous resources have been changed, it is very difficult to tell that from which historical resource the current one evolves.

It is also critical to determine the resources for synchronization. A basic change action performed in an ontology resource probably alters the definitions of others, as a result of synchronization for numerous ontology resources. For instance, the sematics of an ontology class will be changed once the super class is removed.

Visualizing the temporal development of ontology resources is important for facilitating history tracing. To aid the user in recognizing and making sense of the changes, it is critical to visualize the history in a transparent and intuitive manner.

6.4 Theoretical Foundation of the System

The system presented here is designed according to principles of software version control systems to achieve better collaboration support. Users can perform synchronizations between local and shared spaces. Synchronization comprises several basic actions. Committing is used to send a local copy to the repository. Updating is employed to replace a local copy by the one stored in the shared space. When users are working on the same ontology resource at the same time, merging is required. In this section we will introduce the theoretic foundation that supports these actions.

6.4.1 Defining the Level of Granularity for Synchronization

As discussed above, supporting incremental synchronization is vital for our system. To synchronize files incrementally means that only the changed parts of the file need to be exchanged and synchronized. Compared with common text files, where words usually determine the finest level of granularity for incremental synchronization, determining appropriate fine-grained units for an ontology is more complex. Depending on the perspective, different entities can be considered as synchronization units. An ontology can be seen as a set of URIs, a set of nodes and their relations, or a set of triples. Therefore we need to determine an appropriate level of granularity for splitting and synchronizing an ontology.

A viable solution is also required to be easily comprehensible for developers. We will first take a look at how users construct an ontology using graphical editors.

From a semantic point of view, an ontology is set of definitions of domain concepts. Usually an ontology resource represents a domain concept. These ontology resources are classes, properties or slots, individuals or instances. Constructing an ontology is generally a process in which domain experts and knowledge engineers work together to build up these definitions. If we use, for instance, Protége or OntoEdit[69] to develop an ontology, we will see classes and properties listed in a hierarchical tree view. Once we select a concept in the tree, on the right side a editor panel reveals its definition, such as its annotations and its super classes. The concept name together with its definitions are usually the smallest unit that ontology developers are concerned with.

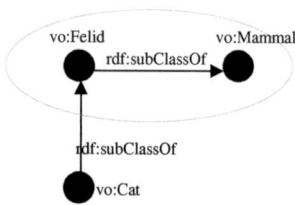

Figure 6.2: the Boundary of Concept *vo:Felid* in the RDF graph

Besides this editor oriented point of view, an ontology can be represented in a RDF graph, which is a set of nodes and their relations. In our case, the amount of information exchanged should be small enough to achieve a high level of efficiency when synchronizing. On the other hand, the information exchanged must still be apprehensible for the ontology developer, and it should support familiar methods of working with development tools and version control systems. It is therefore essential to find a proper mapping between the developers' point of view of ontology resources and the corresponding RDF graph.

Achieving a proper mapping, however, is not straightforward. If we consider a named ontology resource, such as *vo:Felid* in a virtual *Animal* ontology, we can see a corresponding node with URI *'vo:Felid'* as a RDF graph. A single node does not give us any other information for the domain concept *Felid* than its name. However, the task of formalizing domain knowledge is typically related to identifying the right relations between a node and other nodes. For example, we know that *Felid* is a member of *Mammal*, which is represented in the RDF graph as shown in Figure 6.2.

We postulate a first definition of a coherent resource description as follows: Taking a specified resource as a start node, a subgraph including all statements in the source graph where the subject of the statement are the start node can be used to represent a meaningful environment of the resource.

Difficulties are enhanced when there are anonymous nodes in the graph. Anonymous nodes are usually the consequence of using anonymous resources which define

61

common constraints of concepts instead of concepts themselves. For example, we note that all animals of class *Felid* are predators. To represent this situation, we define *Felid* more precisely by stating that "vo:Felid" is a member of the intersection set of "vo:Predator" and "vo:Mammal". We will see this graph in the Figure 6.3.

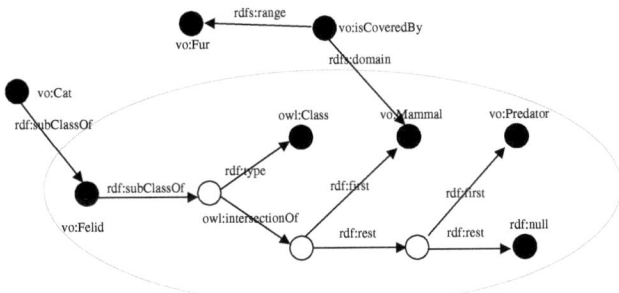

Figure 6.3: the Boundary of Concept *vo:Felid* in RDF graph when there are anonymous nodes in the graph

In order to deal with anonymous nodes we extend our first definition as follows: given a node as starting node, select a subgraph by including

1. all statements in the source graph where the starting node is the the subject of the statement;

2. recursively, for all statements identified in the subgraph thus far having a blank node object, all statements in the source graph where the subject of the statement is the blank node in question and which are not already included in the subgraph.

Our definitions are almost exactly the same as those proposed in Concise Bounded Description(CBD) [56], which is currently a W3C member submission. However, there is a small difference between our definition and CBD, as the definition of CBD also contains content of RDF reifications which is not used in our approach. For the sake of simplicity, we will use the term **CBD** in rest of the thesis.

6.4.2 Detecting Difference after Ontology Modification

The CBD appears to be a suitable foundation for the synchronization given above discussion. Based on a fact that every CBD is always retrieved from a start node and this node must be a named node currently in our case, the system maintains a table of all named nodes and give each one a version number. Since the system maintains a copy both on the local side and on the repository side, we need to track changes happening on the local side, which are caused by users performing modifications in their own work space and which need to be committed to the repository. We also need to detect changes happening on repository side, which are initiated by collaborators who committed their modifications to the repository, and thus need to be retrieved from the server to update the local copy.

If a CBD has been changed by users in the local workspace, we mark its start node as *changedAfterLastSyn*. During synchronization we list all CBDs with this mark and commit them to the repository side. Upon committing, the version number for each CBD will be increased. Modifying an ontology can be seen as a set of basic change operations [37], such as class-equivalence-change etc. A basic change operation will cause changes in one or several triples. Therefore, several nodes may be marked after one basic operation. We developed a mechanism based on monitoring change of statements in the ontology model. Here, two possible situations have to be considered once a statement has been removed or added:

1. The subject of the added(removed) triple is a named node. In this case, we mark this node as *changedAfterLastSyn* in the table.

2. The subject of the added(removed) triple is an anonymous node, or to say, blank node. In this case, we perform the following steps: for the respective triple, use the anonymous subject node as the start node:

   - Step1: include all triples where the object of the triple is the start node;

   - Step2: for each triple obtained in Step1, if the subject is a named node, mark this node as *changedAfterLastSyn* in the table; if the subject is still a anonymous node, define this subject node as starting node and recursively repeat Step1.

While a large part of the basic change operations changes only one triples, such as adding a new super class to current one, there are two distinctive operations which may change multiple triples. These are the actions of renaming and deleting. We will discuss the renaming operation later in sub-section 6.4.4.

Removing a ontology resource means performing a set of actions to modify the RDF graph of the ontology. The triples in which the subject, or object, or prediction is the removed node should be removed. Thus, following the previous definition, a single removing action may cause several ontology resources change their *changedAfterLastSyn* mark.

To detect modified CBDs which need to be retrieved from the repository to update the local copy, we compare the resource version number between local side and repository side. If a node's version number on the repository side is larger than that on the local side, we have to retrieve its CBD content from the repository and replace the one on the local side.

6.4.3 Comparing and Merging Different Ontology Resources

After identifying the CBDs to be synchronized, we have to apply a suitable mechanism for comparing and merging different copies of an ontology resource. This is essential for updating the local model based on the copy on the repository side. First, differences between the local copy and the repository copy must be detected, then a suitable merge method is applied and finally the update is completed.

When two triples contain only named nodes, comparing them is simple. However, comparing two anonymous nodes is more difficult. We cannot detect two anonymous nodes that represent the same domain knowledge by comparing their nodes label. In our system we use a canonical RDF document [15] algorithm. The basic idea of this algorithm is that all triples will be lexicographically sorted and all blank nodes will be deterministically labeled based on their distinctive triples.

From the RDF graph view there are three different merging mechanisms, as shown in figure 6.4[48].

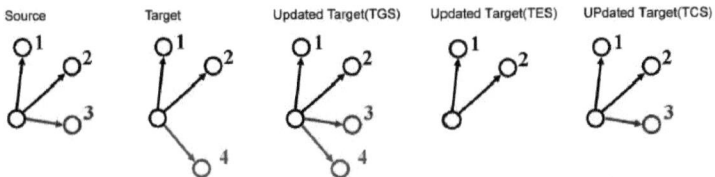

Figure 6.4: Three Different Synchronization Mechanisms

In line with [48] we support all three mechanisms. The mechanism to be used depends on a number of usage scenarios. We distinguish the following scenarios:

1. Using Target Change Sync (TCS) . In this case the local graph will be replaced by the remote graph, since version number of the ontology resource on the repository side is larger then that on the local side. It means that remote users modified the ontology resource and the local model needs to be updated.

2. Using Target Growth Sync (TGS) . In this case, the local graph will be merged with the remote graph. Both the remote and local ontology resource copy have been changed since last synchronization. This creates a *Conflict* in our system, meaning that different users changed the same ontology resource at the same time since the last synchronization.

3. Using Target Erase Sync (TES) . We currently do not use TES to synchronize graphs in our system. However we intend to use it later to offer some management assistance functionalities that will be detailed discussed in the last section.

The merging of ontology resources may destroy the consistency of an ontology. For the sake of the fact that running a consistency check is usually a time-consuming

64

task, we have decided not to include such a mechanism in our implementation. It may not be necessary to perform consistent check every time after synchronization which may be done several times a day. Besides, we are not trying to develop a standard ontology editor but a plugin application for current ontology editors where most of them already offer a consistency checking functionality.

6.4.4 Providing an ID for Each Ontology Resource

There is a special change action - resource **rename**, which may happen frequently during ontology development. It is a simple action with different semantic meanings. Some renaming actions occurred because the name of the resource had spelling mistakes. In this case it is a linguistic happened because the domain concepts changed their names. In this case, a change of semantic meaning may happen. It is very difficult for systems to determine if there are any changes of the semantic meaning behind a renaming action. In our system, we made the assumption that the action of renaming does not create a new resource, it only provides a new name for the existing one. Tracing changes for a resource includes those changes made on the one with the original name. All other resources, which are related with current renamed ones, do not change their version after such rename actions. For example, when the ontology class 'vo:Felid' has been renamed to 'vo:CatLikeAnimals', the semantic meaning of it's children 'vo:Cat' stays still, thus it is not necessary to generate a new version number for 'vo:Cat'.

To implement this approach, we give each named node an ID. The ID is project-unique and stored along with the resource version number. Each named ontology resource in an ontology file has a unique ID. This is reflected in the comparison mechanism used. The comparing mechanism developed takes IDs into account. If two nodes have the same ID but their URI are different, we still regard them as same node. The client side application is responsible for altering the old resource URIs to new URIs for all triples during updating.

```
1. ?<?xml version="1.0" encoding="UTF-8"?>

2. <XMLROOT ID="ROOT">

3. <RepositoryInfo
   RepositoryID="Animal"
   ServiceURL="".../axis2/services/VersioningAxis2Service"
     UserName="Tim" />

4.   <CBDElement
   registeredID="0000000001"
   uri="http://www.uni.Duisburg-Essen.interactivesystems.info/
     OntologyVersioning#ontologyNameSpaceMapElement"
     clientVersionNumber="2.0"
     hasBeenChangedAfterLastSyn="false" />
```

```
5.    <CBDElement registeredID="0000000002"
      uri="http://www.ontoverse.org/namespace#Mammal"
      clientVersionNumber="1.0"
      hasBeenChangedAfterLastSyn="false" />
      .
      .
      .
6.    </XMLROOT>
```

The mapping between ID and URI is stored outside of the ontology model. Currently we stored them in a XML based configuration file and previous code shows the information that the client side application stores. For each named resource, it's URI and current version number will be stored accompany with it's *hasBeenChangedAfterLastSyn* mark as indicated in the paragraph 5. The paragraph 3 saves the connection information of repository, such as Service URL and it's project ID. User information is also written in this paragraph. In order to manage the change of name space in ontologies, a special and virtual ontology resource has been created and there is no such ontology resource in the ontology. The URI of the resource has been defined as 'http://www.uni.Duisburg-Essen.interactivesystems.info/ OntologyVersioning#ontologyNameSpaceMapElement'. All name space related triples will be stored in the CBD of this virtual resource and the ID number of this resource will be always '0000000001', as showing in the paragraph 4.

It is clear that we cannot give anonymous nodes such IDs and store them in a separate file, because anonymous nodes do not have globally unique names in distributed environments. In our system we assume that each anonymous classes [1] is a partial definition of related named classes. The system detects difference between blank nodes following the principle of [15]. Anonymous classes do not maintain a project-unique ID and thus evolution information will be lost.

Besides losing history information for anonymous resources, there is another situation to be considered. It is possible in ontology languages that users construct an anonymous resource and link it to several other named resources. The graph of such situation is shown on the left side of the Figure 6.5. In this graph, the *UnitClass* is, for example, an anonymous ontology class which uses the *owl:unionOf* commend defining that this class is the union of two other named ontology classes. Since we build a resource CBD graph from a start node and this start node is always a named node, it is difficult for us to check if an anonymous class is involved in other CBDs. As a consequence our system will build two identical anonymous resources for each named resource. After reconstructing the ontology from CBD graphs, the system will change the RDF graph slightly as shown on right side of the Figure 6.5. Though the two RDF graphs are isomorphic, there are still some potential risks for ontology developers. For example, modifying the meaning of anonymous class on the left side needs one action, but several actions are required on the right side graph.

---

[1] We will discuss anonymous individuals later in the last session

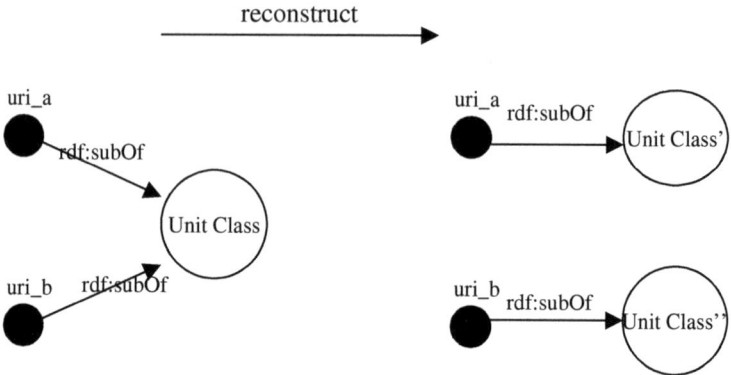

Figure 6.5: left)Original RDF Graph before Reconstructing; right)new RDF graph after reconstructing.

6.5 Prototype System and Use Case for Ontology Versioning

Based on the theoretic foundation given above, we implemented our prototype system to support the ontology versioning control method described above. In this section we introduce our system in detail.

6.5.1 System Overview

The prototype is based on an service-oriented architecture and is independent of concrete editing environments. The entire system can be divided into two parts. The client side part is responsible for managing the local copy of an ontology file. An API is offered to editors for committing ,updating and merging ontology resources. The server side part is responsible for version information storage. There is a set of services offered on the server side based on Axis2 web service container.

While the standard Ontoverse editor is a collaborative ontology editor using a shared workspace, there is one extension version which is a single user editor based on Jena platform. For the current system, we built a plug-in for this single user editor to verify the approach.

6.5.2   A Use Case

The overall process of developing an ontology under the control of ontology versioning system is illustrated by the following scenario. We use the same demo ontology
used in the Chapter 4 to describe our scenario.

The scenario begins when Tim has built a first prototype of the animal ontology
on his local computer. The resources in this prototype are, for example, four classes,
namely *vo:Mammal*, *vo:Predator*, *vo:NonVegetarian* and *vo:Felid*, which is sub-class
of a intersection class of vo:Mammal and vo:Predator. The prototype shows as be-
low (in OWL form):

```
<owl:Class rdf:ID = "Mammal">
</owl:Class>
<owl:Class rdf:ID = "Predator">
</owl:Class>
<owl:Class rdf:ID = "NonVegetarian">
</owl:Class>
<owl:Class rdf:ID = "Felid">
  <rdfs:subClassOf>
    <owl:intersectionOf rdf:parseType="Collection">
      <owl:Class rdf:resource = "Mammal">
      <owl:Class rdf:resource = "Predator">
    </owl:intersectionOf>
  </rdfs:subClassOf>
</owl:Class>
```

To start a collaboration, Tim shares his ontology with his collaborators through
the shared repository. He knows that the ontology versioning system is running on a
server and the service end point reference(EPR) is, for instance, *www.ontologyshare.de/
services/ OntologyVersioningServices*. He opens the **Versioning** tabpage of the editor and sets up a connection with the help of a configuration wizard. He creates a
new project in the wizard and names it as *AnimalOntology*. Some comments may
also be given at that time. When the wizard finishes, the editor is ready to commit
the four classes created locally to the repository.

Now the animal ontology is under the control of ontology version system. On
the client side, the four classes created are now each associated with the resource
version number *1.0*.

When Tim's colleague Lang wants to start work on the animal ontology, he first
needs to retrieve the initial ontology version from the repository. With the help of
the configuration wizard Lang chooses the *AnimalOntology* project and downloads
the classes from the repository.

At 13:00, Tim adds a new definition of *Mammal*. He defines that mammals
have fur by adding a new property *vo:isCoveredBy* and a new class *vo:Fur*. Lang
changes the definition of *felid* at 14:00 by defining it as a subclass of both mammal

and non-vegetarian. Now the table in Lang's computer will mark the ontology class vo:Felid as *changeAfterLastSyn*. 14:10 Lang finishes his synchronization with the repository. The ontology class vo:Felid will be committed to the repository and its version number will be set to *2.0*. Tim synchronizes again at 14:30. After clicking the synchronize button, three ontology resources will be listed.

In the editor Tim now sees that the two new ontology resources, *vo:isCov-eredBy*, *vo:Fur*, created by him need to be committed to the repository. He is also aware of the change Lang applied to the ontology resource *vo:Felid*. He clicks the resource to see detailed information. On the comparison panel on the right-hand side he notices that the super class definition has been changed. Moreover, he knows the reason of modification since Lang wrote some comments. By clicking the 'CommitUpdate' button, the system will commit two resources to the repository and load one from the server and replace the local copy. Now both ontologies located on Tim's local computer and the repository contain five ontology resources with version number 1.0, which are *vo:Mammal*, *vo:isCoveredBy*, *vo:Fur*, *vo:Predator* and *vo:NonVegetarian*, and one resource, which is *vo:Felid*, with version number 2.0. The ontology shows as following:

```
<owl:Class rdf:ID = "Mammal">            //version 1.0
</owl:Class>
<owl:ObjectProperty rdf:ID = "isCoveredBy"> //version 1.0
  <rdfs:domain rdf:resource = "Mammal">
  <rdfs:range rdf:resource = "Fur">
</owl:DatatypeProperty>
<owl:Class rdf:ID = "Fur">                //version 1.0
</owl:Class>
<owl:Class rdf:ID = "Predator">          //version 1.0
</owl:Class>
<owl:Class rdf:ID = "NonVegetarian">     //version 1.0
</owl:Class>
<owl:Class rdf:ID = "Felid">             //version 2.0
  <rdfs:subClassOf>
    <owl:intersectionOf rdf:parseType="Collection">
      <owl:Class rdf:resource = "Mammal">
      <owl:Class rdf:resource = "NonVegetarian">
    </owl:intersectionOf>
  </rdfs:subClassOf>
</owl:Class>
```

Different copies of ontology resources will be stored on the repository. The system also stores necessary versioning information, such as who has made the modification and when is the modification get done. This information will be used to generated representation of changes discussed in next sub-section. Some important information stored on the repository is shown in the Table 6.1.

URI	Vn	CBD	User	Time	Comment
Vo:Mammal	1.0	xml graph...	Tim	12:00	...prototype...
Vo:Fur	1.0	xml graph...	Tim	14:30	...all mammal...
Vo:Felid	1.0	xml graph...	Tim	12:00	...prototype...
Vo:Felid	2.0	xml graph...	Lang	14:10	... sub of...

Table 6.1: Version Information Stored on the Repository

We give each ontology resource a version number, namely *Resource Version Number* or *Rv* in short. Meanwhile, our system also supports attaching version number to ontology, named as *Ontology Version Number* or *Ov*. For example Tim could generate the first ontology version after he built up the prototype. In this case ontology version number 1.0 is composed of four ontology classes and each one is identified as resource version number 1.0. After modification made by both Tim and Lang, a second ontology version can be generated. Ontology version number 2.0 contains six ontology resources and one of them, vo:Felid, has resource version number 2.0. Table 6.2 and Table 6.3 show how to store these ontology version information on the repository.

ResourceURI	ResourceVn
vo:Mammal	1.0
vo:Predator	1.0
vo:NonVegetarian	1.0
vo:Felid	1.0
/	/
/	/

Table 6.2: Resources in ontology V1.0

ResourceURI	ResourceVn
vo:Mammal	1.0
vo:Predator	1.0
vo:NonVegetarian	1.0
vo:Felid	2.0
vo:Fur	1.0
vo:isCoveredBy	1.0

Table 6.3: Resources in ontology V2.0

6.5.3 Version management on the client application

Based on the single user model of the Ontoverse editor, a special component has been implemented and embedded into the editor. The component was designed to manage the versioning information on the client side and also it will detect which resources need to be committed to the repository. Several icons were imported to the editor and a wizard window has been developed which helps users manage their connection with the repositories.

The existence of private workspaces in our system is the unique feature different from many other ontology editors. There is no requirements that all users need to be online when they are working together. Online connection is only required when users want to synchronize their ontologies to the shared repository.

In order to contribute private ontologies to the repository, necessary information, such as where is the repository located and what is the name of current users, need to be entered into the system. A wizard window was implemented to help users manage such information. The first information that users need to input is the name and the EPR of the repository service. The system will valid the EPR and store it into the XML file.

Every development of an ontology is represented as a project in the system. A project needs an identification to indicate itself. One of the wizard windows help users create or join projects. Users could create new project by clicking the 'create new project' button and inputting the project identification and description. Time and creator information will be automatically stored together with identification.

Another option for users is that they can join an existing project. Usually users will join the project from 'zero', which means they join the project before they start to contribute their own working into the ontology. The system will download all existing ontology resources from the repository and build up a copy on the client side. Users need to define the file name and path in which the ontology will be stored. A helper file which stores other versioning information for each ontology resource will be automatically generated and saved in the same path.

However, it is not obligatory that users join the project from 'zero'. Another possibility supported by the system is that the users could build their own prototype ontologies on the private workspaces before they start to join a project. Conflicts determination will be performed in this case. After download all existing ontology resources from the repository, the system determines conflicts by comparing the URI of each resource. When a local copy of a ontology resource shares a same URI with the server side one, the system defines this ontology resource's status as *'conflict'* and the user need to manage it. Currently the system will merge two copy following the TGS 6.4.3 method.

The interface of the editor will indicate to users if the local ontology is under control of the versioning system. There are two kinds of icons used to indicate the current versioining status of the resources if the ontology is already controlled by the ontology version system. One icon beside the class hierarchy indicates that the ontology resources are controlled and have not been locally changed since last synchronization. Another icon which is marked with a pencil indicates that the resources have been changed by the users and need to be committed to the repository. Detailed information, such as version number and versioning ID for the resource, can be viewed if users hover mouse point over the icons.

Currently, users will not be aware of the situation, that the ontology resources have been changed by other users. Such limit comes from the fact that the repository service is build upon the Web Service technique. In the HTTP protocol it is difficult that services **push** data to the client applications. Possible solutions will be discussed in the last chapter 8.

An GUI for ontology synchronization was implemented to help users synchronize their local copies with the repository. To use such functionality, users need to firstly compare the difference in copies between client side and repository side by clicking 'synchronization' button. Comparison will be performed to check the version number stored both on local side and the repository side. Four kinds of differences will be found and listed, there are:

1. **Local Creation.** When the local user created new ontology resources, these resources need to get their identification from the server and commit to the repository for the first time.

2. **Local modification.** The identification of these resources have already been assigned. The 'hasBeenChangedAfterLastSyn' status has been set as true indicating that the resources have been edited. The system will commit these resources to the repository and then an increased version number will be reassigned to each resources.

3. **Collaborative modification.** When the version number stored on the repository side is larger then the one on the local side, the system detects that other users changed the resource and committed. The system will download the CBD information from the server and change the local copy. The version number on the local side will be replaced by the repository one.

4. **Conflict.** Conflicts will be detected when on the one hand the local status of 'hasBeenChangedAfterLastSyn' is true, on the other hand the version number on the repository side is larger then the local one. The local user and a collaborative user changed the same ontology resource in the same time. Currently an automatically merging will be used and triples both in the CBDs of the local copy and the repository copy will be merged to create a new resource. The version number will be increased both on the client side and the repository side.

The Figure 6.6 shows a snapshot of the screen after the system has compared the two versions. On the left side of the window there is a Tree component used to indicate which resources need to be synchronized with the repository. Different icons indicate the corresponding difference types. For example the icon with green arrow indicates that the local resource has been changed and will be committed to the repository.

Users usually want to see the difference between two copies of the resource. The system will illustrate the content of the CBD information of the copies in two tree components located on the right side of the GUI. The local copy will be displayed on the left side tree component and the tree component on the right hand side shows the copy from the repository side. Each line (tree node, except the first root line) corresponds to a triple and is displayed by two icons and corresponding text. The property in the triple will be displayed by the first icon and text and the object is illustrated by the second icon and text. All tree nodes in the same level share the same subject which is the object of the parent tree nodes. We use the tree structure to show the anonymous resource structure. Users need to notice that we changed slightly the representation for anonymous resource which uses collection structure, such as using of 'rdf:first' and 'rdf:next'. These properties will be replaced by an virtual property *'members'* thus two lists with same contents but different sequences will be judged as equal.

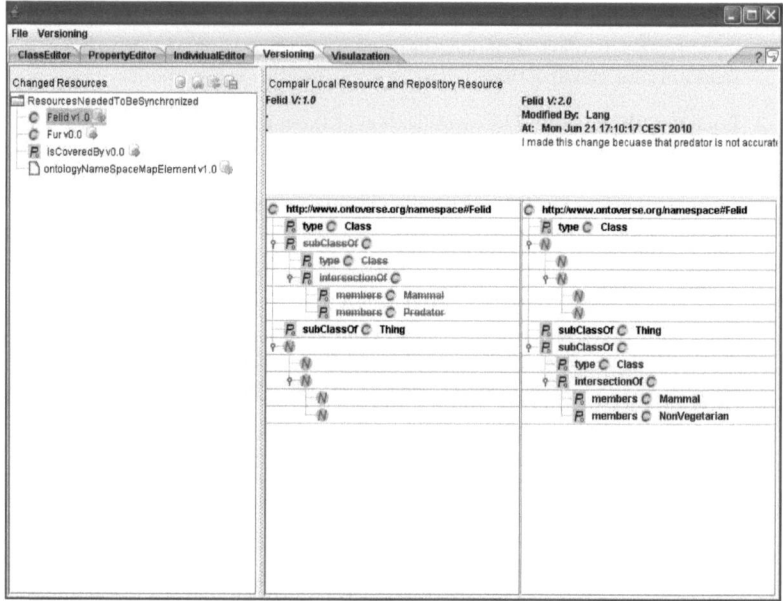

Figure 6.6: The synchronazation GUI for users

A 'CommitAndUpdate' button is used to synchronize the local ontology copy with the repository. Currently the system does not support users in synchronizing only a part of the ontology. The connections among different ontology resources are extremely complicated and partial synchronization may raise serious inconsistency problems. For example if a user only synchronize the deleted class 'vo:Felid' in the demo ontology and does not synchronize its children, such as 'vo:Cat'. Errors will be occurred when other users make their synchronization. In this case the class of 'vo:Cat' contains an invalid triple, such as 'vo:Cat rdf:subClassOf vo:Felid', because there is no such parent class in the ontology anymore.

During commiting and updating, a potential user error may happen. It will be raised in the following sequence. Two users changed the same ontology resource, for example 'vo:Cat', and click 'Synchronization' button in almost the same time. The copy of each 'vo:Cat' will be compared to the current shared one on the repository. A user commits his change quite soon because there is only a few resources have been changed. Thus the copy of 'vo:Cat' on the repository has been replaced and version number has been increased. Another user commits his change now and the system will tell him that ontology class of 'vo:Cat' has been just renewed and he has to synchronize with the latest version again. If not then the dangerous dirty-writing will be performed so that the copy of the first user will be overwritten without any comparison.

6.5.4 Visualization of Ontology Evolution

Representing changes in an intuitive way is an important task in ontology evolution. A good visualization enables users to understand the temporal context of the ontology alongside the development process. However, the study of ontology change representations is still in an early stage. Some applications offer change logs, while others provide a table of changed resources for two different ontology versions. In this system we try to present users with a more intuitive interface to understand the location, type and time context of changes, not only for different ontology versions, but also for different resource versions. Figure 6.7 shows the corresponding user interface.

On the left-most side, a tree component shows resources in a hierarchical structure. The visualization uses a *SmartTree* component. As mentioned in the previous chapter, the relevance of the nodes can be flexibly determined by the application. In this system, resources that were modified are considered *important* nodes. Once nodes are set to 'important', users can *shrink* the tree by clicking a button beside the root node, or a parent node. A shrinked tree indicates only those nodes, that are either important, or have important children. All other nodes will be hidden. Users can *expand* the shrinked tree at any time. They can expand either the whole tree, or a particular sub-tree. By providing this focus-and-context visualization, the user can easily perceive modified resources while maintaining an overview of the complete class structure which may be very large.

In order to use the interface, users need to list all generated ontology versions first. Then the versions will be listed in the upper right list component, and users can choose one as a *base point*. The system will construct a hierarchical resource structure in the SmartTree component. Initially, no nodes are set as important. Then users can choose another version as a *reference* version. The system will then list all modifications, including altered resources, newly created resources and removed resources, and mark them as important nodes in the tree component. Different colors and font styles are employed to indicate different types of modifications. Nodes with blue color indicate that they have been altered between base and target version. Nodes with red color indicate that these nodes are newly created in the target version and do not exist in base version. Those resources which have been removed in the target version will be printed in gray and crossed out. A list of changed nodes will be also printed on a list component on the upper middle area of the window. This list also indicates some additional information about the changes. For instance, users may notice that the resource version number of a ontology resource has been changed from Rv1.0 to Rv2.0. All unchanged resources will be hidden automatically in the tree. Users can always expand the tree at any time to see the complete structure or complete subtrees. The features discussed are shown in Figure 6.7.

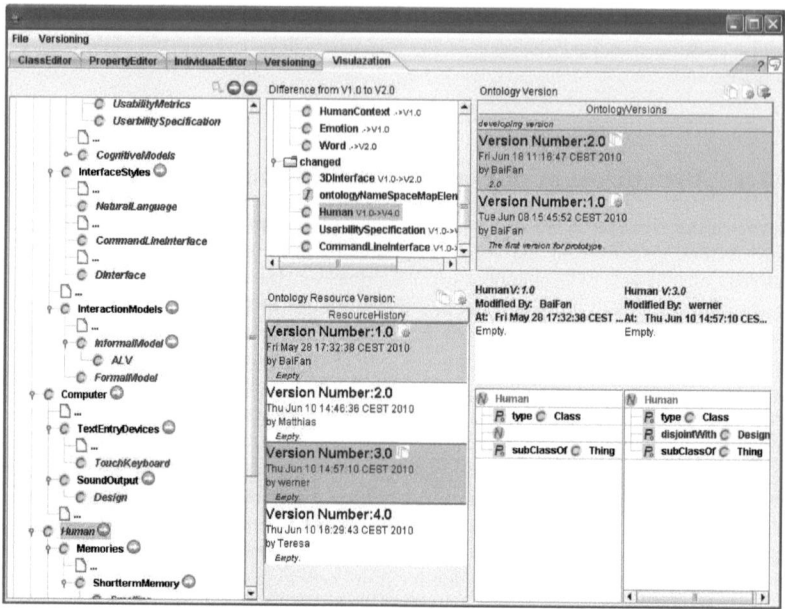

Figure 6.7: GUI for Representing Changes between Two Ontology Versions

History information for a particular ontology resource will be loaded in the right bottom area. Users can list all history versions of a resource by choosing an ontology resource and clicking the *Show History* button. Like comparing different ontology versions, resource versions can be compared likewise. Comparisons are performed between a base and a reference resource version chosen by the user. The left tree shows triples of resources in the base version, the right tree shows triples in the reference version. Sub-trees are used to indicate complex classes. Same color and font strategy is selected here. Since we assume that there is no *alteration* in triples, while a node alternation occurred in any place in a triple causes creation of a new triple and deletion of the old one, blue color is printed to highlight the difference.

Our system offers users a static view of the changes that happened between two different versions, either ontology versions or resource versions. Users can thus understand what was changed between two versions. However, they cannot be aware of how these changes were made during the development. For example, a comment for vo:Felid might be 'Felids are cat-like animals.' in resource version 1.0. At a later stage, the user might see a comment 'They are cat-like animals, and they all eat meat.' in resource version 5.0. The user might think that this was caused by editing the old comment, whereas in fact the old comment was removed in resource version 2.0 and a new comment was added in 4.0. To understand precise sequence of changes we need other supports, such as change logs.

Chapter 7

Architecture and Implementation

In this chapter we will discuss the software architecture and the implementation of the applications. Detailed information, such as how events are distributed among different software components, or what are the main functions for certain Java classes, will be presented with the help of UML diagrams. By the fact of large size of the applications, it is hard and also not necessary to discuss the implementation for every classes or functions. The class diagrams as well as sequence diagrams used to demonstrate the system are simplified, e.g. some parameters or methods are ignored or some components are not involved.

7.1 Collaborative Ontology Development Environment - Ontoverse Editor

As mentioned in chapter 6, the Ontoverse editor is based on the SWAT platform and provides users a group-aware environment where they could interactively and collaboratively develop ontologies. Some major features include, and are not limited to, group-awareness, lock mechanism and the *SmartTree* visualization. While the description of the entire application implementation is beyond the scope of the thesis, we will focus on several key features and discuss how they have been developed.

7.1.1 Application Architecture

The Ontoverse editor can be divided into four layers. The first layer is responsible for data visualization and controls editing operations, such as adding a new ontology class or renaming an existing ontology resource. They are the *VIEW* and *CONTROL* components in the application. The second layer acts as a *MODEL* component and controls data modification of ontologies. Between the *SWAT* platform and the *MODEL* component, there is an *Adapter* layer. This layer supports us in employing other platforms or ontology API, such as Jena ontology API, besides the SWAT platform. Fig 7.1 illustrates the application architecture.

76

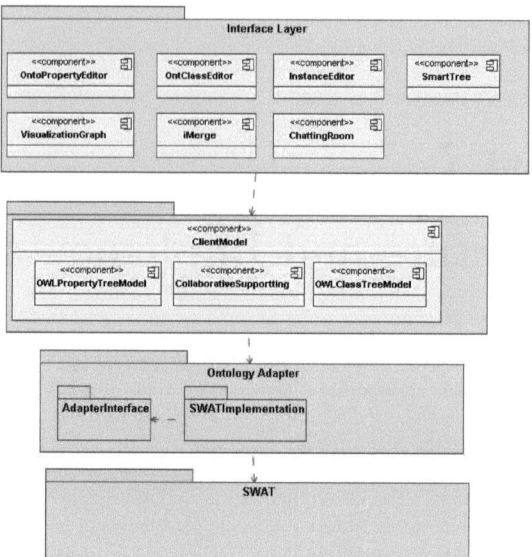

Figure 7.1: The Architecture of the Ontoverse Editor

In the first layer, several components have been implemented. The *SmartTree* component is developed to support advanced visualization for large quantity of contents in a standard tree component. It serves to display class and property taxonomy of the editing ontology. *ClassEditor*, *PropertyEditor* as well as *InstanceEditor* are the major components, which support ontology modification in a graphical interface. A list of buttons located on these components supports basic editing operations, such as adding new classes and removing properties. Beside the editors, the *VisualizationGraph* was developed to illustrate ontology into graphs. Currently, the **Morcego** and **TouchGraph** visualization mechanisms have been embedded. The *ChattingRoom* component provides a instance communication channel which helps users keep in touch when they are working together.

The second layer is made of application models. Editing operations performed by users will change the data in the model. Hence, a couple of functions have been developed to support these operations. For instance, the function *createNewNamed-Class(String URI)* creates a new ontology class with URI. And in order to illustrate class and property taxonomy on the interface, the tree models will be established when users open an ontology file. The *CollaborativeSupporting* model serves to control the distribution of collaborative events and display them on GUI.

Above the *SWAT* platform, we build adapter components. These components isolate the detailed implementation of underlying platforms from the upper level components, so that we can use different platforms or ontology API. Currently we have developed an implementation supporting SWAT platform and another implementation supporting Jena ontology API.

7.1.2 Implementation of the SmartTree

Tree components are widely used to express taxonomy structure of ontologies. The amount of content of an ontology is variable, from hundreds of resources to ten thousands of resources. It is difficult for users to maintain an overview and to navigate to a specific node in the tree when the number of nodes becomes very large. The **SmartTree** component was developed to overcome such limitations of the standard tree component, it helps users find interesting information from very large amount of content. A innovative features is that users can hide unimportant nodes in the tree and only important information will be displayed.

The SmartTree component is based on the standard Java tree component in the Swing platform and contains over ten different Java classes and approximately 3000 lines of code. In this section we will discuss only those that are most important in supporting *spread* and *shrink* functions. The *shrink* function removes un-important nodes from the tree visualization and replaces the hidden nodes with a special nodes indicating that some nodes have been removed. The *spread* function makes those hidden nodes visible again. The standard Java tree component and how can it be drawn on the screen will be explained in the first place. And then we will introduce how we extend the standard version to generate the SmartTree component.

The implementation of the components of the Swing platform, such as a JButton or a JTable component, follows the principle of MVC model. In this model there are three parts, *Model*, *Controll* and *Visualization*. The *Model* part is utilized to contain the content to be expressed; The *Controlling* part is responsible for managing the behavior of the component, for example how a component should react when a user click it; The *Visualization* part defines how to draw it on the screen.

Overview of the Tree Component

Fig 7.2 shows the class diagram in UML of the standard tree component. Following the MVC model, three classes, *TreeModel*[1], *JTree* as well as *BasicTreeUI* , were developed to implement the tree component in the Swing platform. *TreeModel* will be build up by software developers and it contains the content which should be displayed on the screen. *TreeNode* is the unit that is used to build such tree model and software developers define the filiation between TreeNodes. *JTree* is responsible for controlling the tree component and reacting the user actions, such as expanding the children or collapsing a parent node. The Swing platform supports different, pluggable representations of the same component so that it can be drawn in different

[1]In the Swing platform, it is a interface. We call it class in order to simplify the description

styles. The *BasicTreeUI* is the standard visualization of the tree component and defines the basic appearance of the tree in the Java environment.

While the SmartTree component changes primarily the UI(User Interface) part of the Java tree component, the detailed implementation of which will be discussed. In the standard tree UI class, a rectangle will be drawn on the screen to define the area of the tree component. Inside this area contents of the model, which are the TreeNodes in the tree model, will be represented as string format with an icon in lines. The first line is usually used to represent the root node of the tree, and the children nodes will be drawn underneath with indent. A horizontal line will be presented in the left side of the children nodes to clearly identify the scope of the children. A plus sign with border in the left side of the node string reports that this node contains children.

Coordination Calculation

In order to visualize the tree model in such mode, it is necessary to know the coordination among each node so as to display them in the accurate place. The BasicTreeUI class uses the *JavaVariableHeightLayoutCache*, which uses a tree model object that assists UI class to calculate the position of each line of content. The *TreeStateNode* implemented the *TreeNode* interface is the unit of the *JavaVariableHeightLayoutCache* that contains the coordinate of each content inside the tree model. Once a tree model is built and about to be illustrated on the screen, the UI class will receive the model and retrieve the content. In the first phase it only retrieves the root node, the first layer as children from the tree model. Each node in the tree model will be wrapped into the corresponding *TreeStateNode*. From the first line of the tree, which is the root node with coordinate (x=0, y=0)[2], the *JavaVariableHeightLayoutCache* calculates the coordinate of each *TreeStateNode* and assigns the number into the attributes. The calculation can be simplified as follows: the start position is the upper-left position of the line, where the first line is defined as (x=0,y=0). Based on that, the second line will be (0+indent*1, 0+Height(root)), and the third line will then be (0+indent*1,0+Height(root)+Height(SecondNode)), and so forth. In this mechanism, the start position of a given node can be calculated from following formula:

$P_x = Indent * Deep;$
$P_y = \sum_{i=0}^{y-1} Height(Node_i)$

The *Indent* is the constant number and used to define the space that the child node should indent comparing to its parent node. The *Deep* is the number of ancestors the current node has. While the *JavaVariableHeightLayoutCache* supports variable height of nodes, we need to summarize the height of all previous lines to determine the current horizontal coordination.

---

[2]It is not zero in the practical case but we use zero to simplify the discussion

79

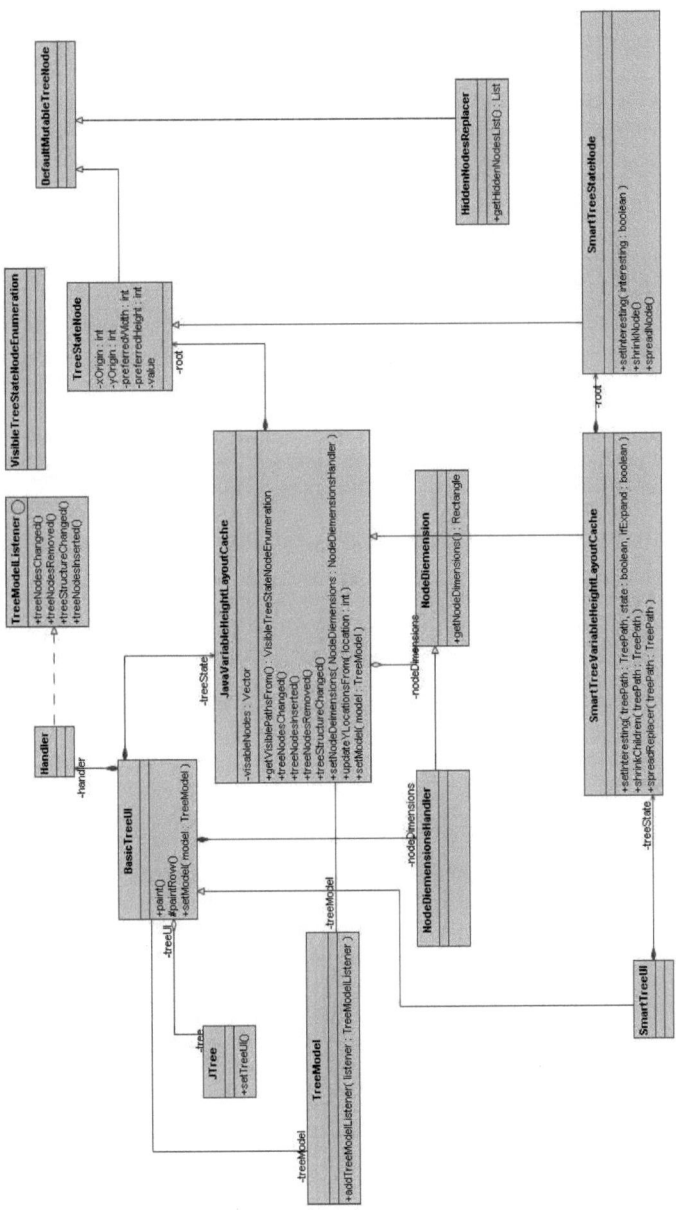

Figure 7.2: The Important Classes for the Implementation of the SmartTree

To calculate the horizontal coordination of the given node, it is key to know how many nodes have been printed in the previous rows. The *JavaVariableHeightLayoutCache* contains an Vector object to manage the visible tree nodes. The subscript of the vector indicates the number of line for its content. With the help of such vector, named as *visiableNodes*, and the *JavaVariableHeightLayoutCache* object the UI component determines which tree nodes are visible and which coordinations they possess.

Expand and Collapse

The *expand* and *collapse* functions are not only the basic requirements for a tree component, but also the basis for our *spread* and *shrink* functions. Detailed implementation enables us to design and execute the extension components.

Both functions are triggered by users, for example users double click on an unexpanded parent node so that its children underneath will be disclosed. Collapsing is the inverse action and makes those child nodes invisible.

Fig 7.3 shows a flow diagram for the expand function, indicating the calculations performed when the function is triggered. The tree component needs to retrieve the child nodes from the model and wrap them into the *JavaVariableHeightLayoutCache*, so that all child nodes will be inserted into the *visibleNodes* vector. The horizontal coordination of all relative nodes, including inserted child nodes and existed nodes located underneath, will be re-calculated by operating the mechanism discussed before. The implementation of the collapsing function is the inverse flow that the child nodes will be removed from the *visibleNodes* vector.

Painting Component on the Screen

The major task for the UI component is to paint the components on the screen. During the *paint()* method, which is triggered by the computer system where a window is shown on the screen, the tree UI component will firstly reveal a rectangle area on the screen. This area is the range and scope where the tree is displayed.

Fig 7.4 indicates the flow diagram of the painting method and its result. By applying the *VisibleTreeStateNodeEnumeration*, all the visible tree nodes inside the rectangle area can be enlisted. The tree UI component reveals each tree node step by step.

The SmartTree Extension

As illustrated in the Fig 7.2, three extensions, *SmartTreeUI*, *SmartTreeVariableHeightLayoutCache* and *SmartTreeStateNode*, were developed to support *Shrink* and

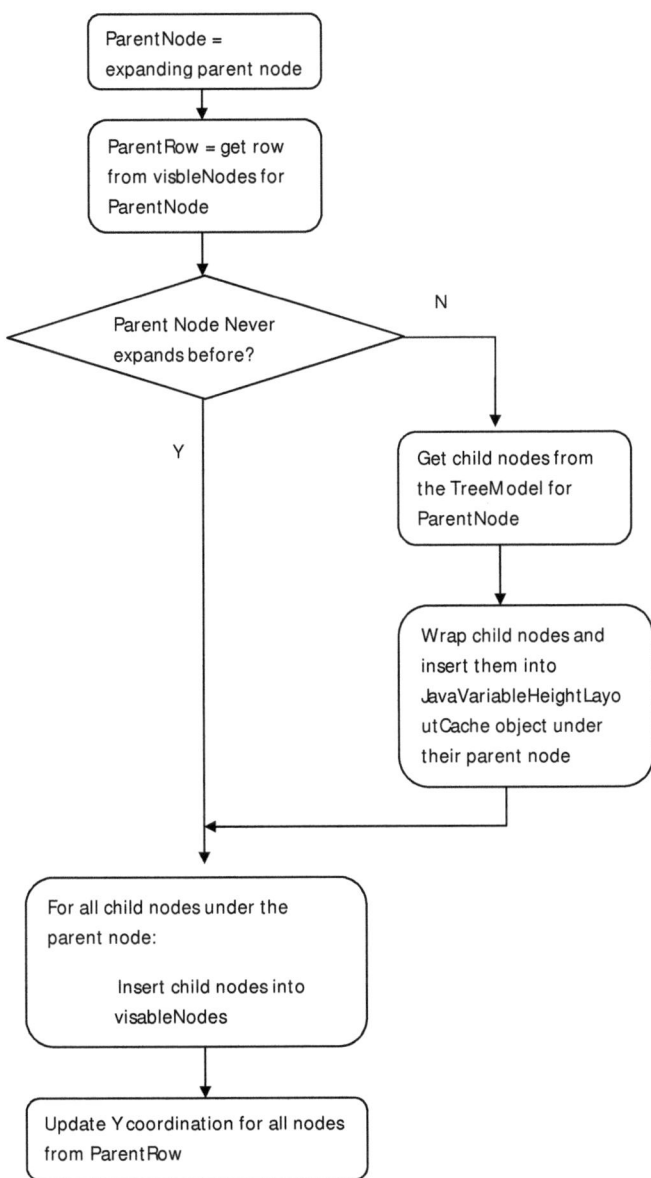

Figure 7.3: The Flow Diagram of Expand Function

82

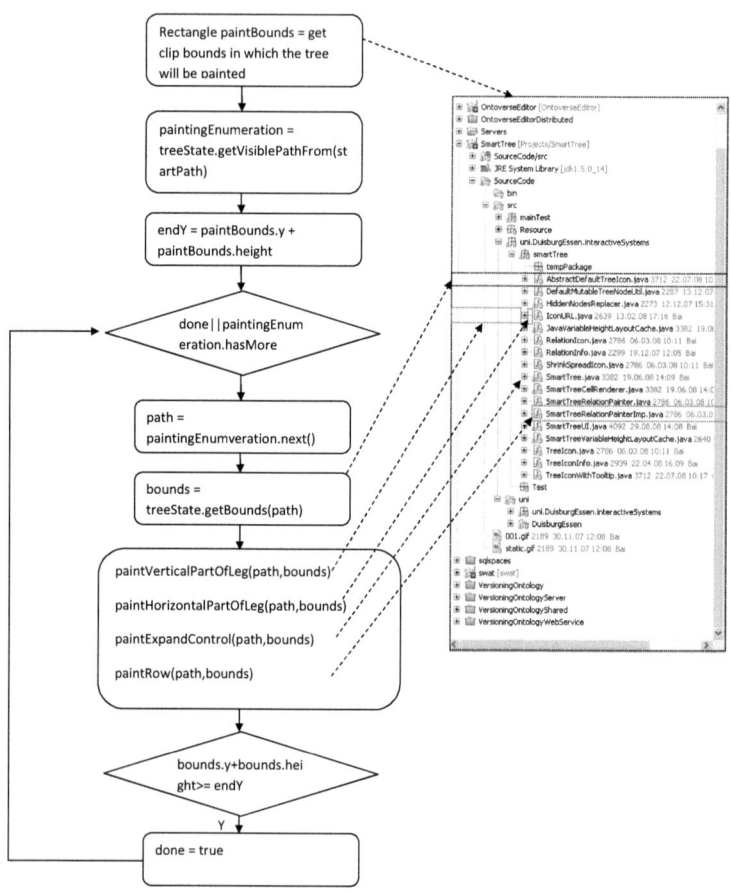

Figure 7.4: Paint a Tree on the Screen

Spread functions. The implementation of them are similar to the expand and collapse functions discussed before.

In the class of *SmartTreeStateNode* we developed three primary methods to support the Shrink/Spread functions:

1. setInteresting() method: under this method, we define that current tree node is important and users have interest in viewing it. This node should be painted always on the screen. Once a child node is set as important node, all its parent nodes will be automatically set as important nodes in order to maintain the tree structure on the screen.

2. shrinkNode() method: the triggering of this method will remove all the child nodes which were not set as important. In other word, they will not be painted by the UI component on the screen. The unimportant nodes will firstly be removed from the *SmartTreeVariableHeightLayoutCache* and then from the *visibleNodes* vector. If the removed nodes are located in a consecutive rank, they will be replaced by a *HiddenNodesReplacer* object, which will be displayed on the screen as a blank node representing the removed nodes. Fig 7.5 demonstrates the flow diagram of the method.

3. spreadNode() method: inverse of the shrinkNode() method, which removes the replacer node and resumes removed nodes to their ordinary position. The removed nodes will be added back into the *SmartTreeVariableHeightLayout-Cache* and the *visibleNodes* vector. The position of each node will be recalculated. Fig 7.6 illustrates the flow diagram.

While the functions were primarily based on the *SmartTreeStateNode*, we also developed several methods so that users could easily apply the features offered by the SmartTree component. For example, instead of spreading only the current node, the *spreadNodeAll()* method will spread all child nodes which were shrunk before. Due to the page limitation of this thesis, we will not go too deeply in studying those methods.

7.1.3 Implementation of Cooperative Awareness

In the editor, the implementation of the cooperative awareness includes several functions, such as, group-awareness, locking mechanism, chatting etc. They share a similar implementation process. We will give one example in this sections to clarify how these functions are implemented. Firstly, the class diagram will be enlisted and verified. Then we will lay out two sequence diagram to describe how these components interact with each other.

Class Diagram

As discussed in the subsection 7.1.1, the editor is based on the *SWATClient* platform. We build an adapter layer between the SWATClient platform and the application

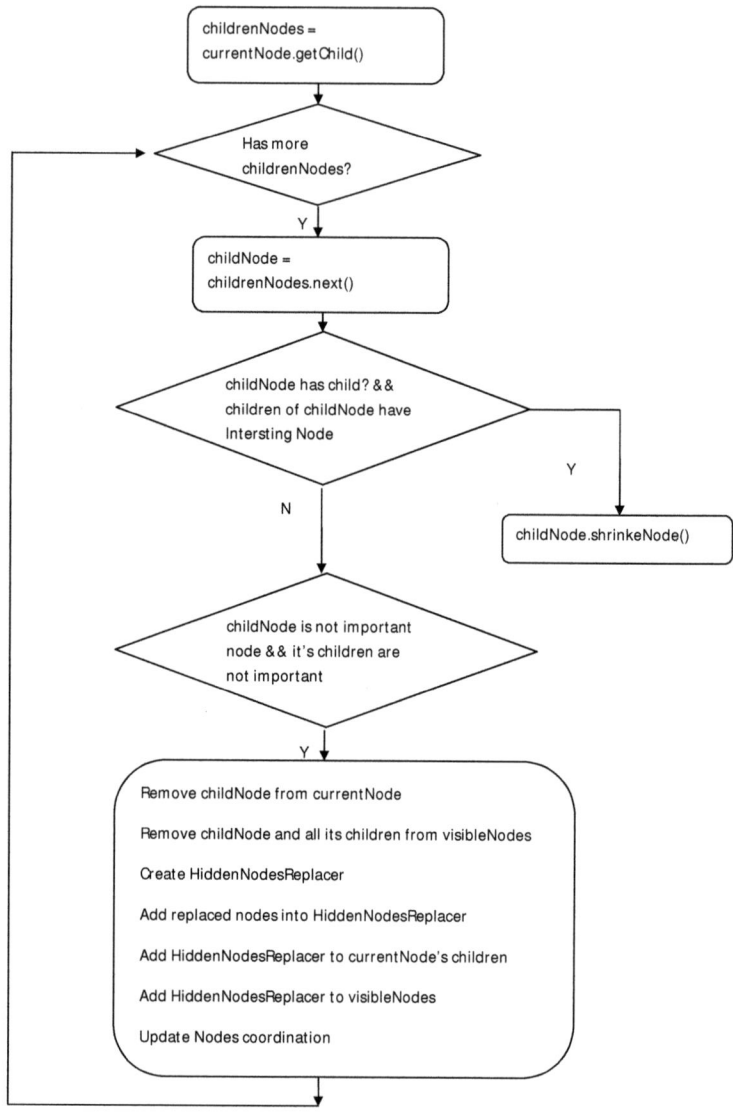

Figure 7.5: Shink Function: remove the unimportant nodes from the visualization of the tree component.

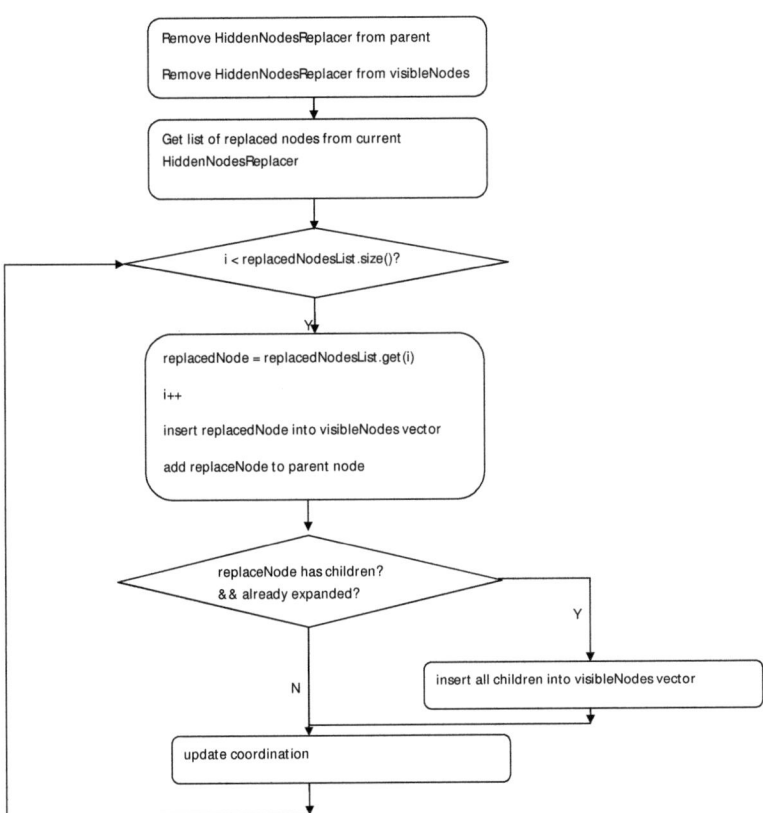

Figure 7.6: Spread Functions: inverse of Shink function, resume the hidden unimportant nodes to their ordinary position.

model layer to increase the feasibility of the editor. The existence of this layer makes it possible for us to switch our editor to different platforms and ontology APIs. However, this layer increased the complexity of the structure and the implementation, especially in supporting cooperative event listening.

A set of classes has been designed and implemented to support users editing ontology resources under the control of lock, Fig 7.7 shows the class diagram.

The *ClientModel* class is the model object for the entire editor. It contains the data of the editing ontology and offers a set of methods to access the data, such as creating a new ontology class and inserting it into the class taxonomy tree structure. The interface *OntModel* is the attribute of the ClientModel and serves to represent the ontology API or platform. The application of **Interface** isolates the detailed implementation underneath. This interface acts as a *Adapter* layer between the client model layer and the ontology API layer. Several standard methods were identified within the interface, for example, the method *createOntClass()* will create an ontology class entity in the ontology. The implementation of such creation access will be realized by different classes. For instance, the *OntModelTSImpl* class implemented the interface and use *SWATClient.doOperation()* method with a parameter of an operation bean to create a new ontology class in the ontology space.

The *CooperativeInfo* interface provides cooperation support functions for the editor, such as group-awareness supporting, lock mechanism supporting as well as chatting functions. Performing the interface allows us to employ different mechanisms to implement such functions. In the SWAT platform we use embedded cooperation support. We can also build other implementations based on CORBA or Web Service platform to offer similar functions. The implementation of the interface is *CooperativeInfoTSImpl*. While the cooperative operations are already supported on the SWAT platform, the class *OntModelTSImpl* containing the instance of the SWAT client will trigger the listener of *OntModelCooprativeListener* when cooperation events have been received. The class *CooperativeInfoTSImpl* will then analysis the SWAT cooperation events and interprete these events to application standard events and finally transfer them to upper layer users, such as a listener registered by ontology class editor GUI.

The *SWATClient* class and the *AwareComponent* interface offers the editing and cooperative awareness functions based on the SWAT platform. They are the client side application of the platform. Detailed discussion of SWAT platform will not be presented in this thesis.

Sequence Diagram of the Lock Mechanism

The lock mechanism is one of the most important features supported by the editor. The lock determines that only one user can modify the ontology resource at any time. Potential modifiers need to wait before the current user finishes his modification and releases the lock. The ontology resource assigned with a lock will be

87

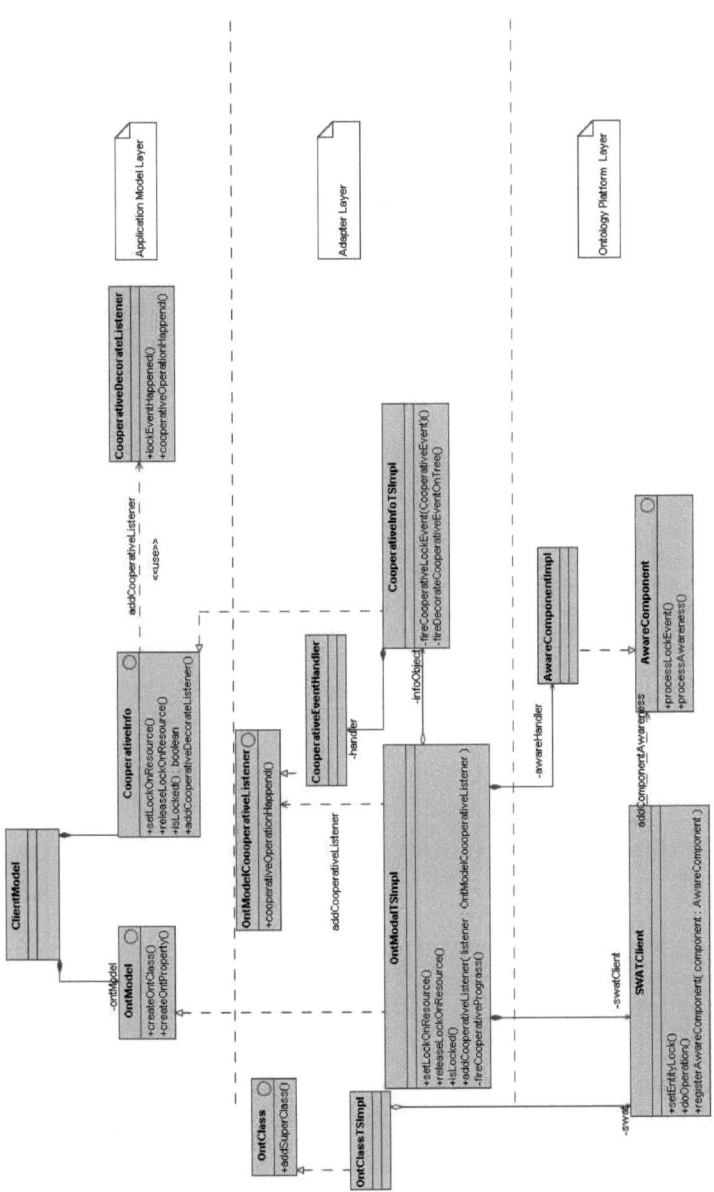

Figure 7.7: The List of the Classes Used to Supporting Cooperation Awareness

represented in the editor GUI with a lock icon indicating current lock state. The implementation of such mechanism is representative. Other functions, such as chatting, follow the similar process.

The implementation can be divided into two phases. The first phase is the sender-phase. In this phase a ontology developer edits the ontology so that the system generates the editing events and sends events to the other editors. The second phase is the receive-phrase. The system receives the editing events and demonstrates the events on the screen.

We give an example of adding new super class to an existed ontology class to denote how the system implement the lock mechanism. Fig 7.8 indicates the sequence diagram of the first phase. In this phase four application components(classes) are included.

1. **setLockOnResource**() method: This method will set a lock on the given ontology resource. The resource with a lock can only be modified by lock owner. This method is application standard method and acts as an adapter layer. The class *CooperativeInfoTSImpl* implements the *CooperativeInfo* interface and delivers the *setLockOnResource()* method to *OntModelTSImpl* to process the lock setting function.

2. **setLockOnResource**() method: Since the SWAT client offer the cooperative supporting so that all functions, including modifying functions and cooperative functions, were wrapped in the *OntModelTSImpl* class. This class translates the application standard methods, such as set lock method to SWAT platform standard methods. The method offered by SWAT platform dealing with lock setting is *setEntityLock()*. This class invokes such method and informs SWAT platform that on the given ontology resource a lock will be set up.

3. **setEntityLock**() method: This is a method offered by SWAT platform. It adds a command in the session space and distributes the lock setting event to all participated clients.

4. **addSuperClass**() method: The invocation of such method will be triggered by users though clicking on a function button on the GUI. By clicking this button, users are entitled to define the super classes of given ontology class and to view the class displayed at the proper position in the class taxonomy. The parameters of this method are the URI of the super class which inputed by users. The newly created ontology class should be indicated under the parent class in the ontology class hierarchical structure. Before the invocation of the method to modify class in the ontology file, this method invokes the *setLockOnResource()* method first to validate that only one user could modify the class. It is a standard application method which acts as an adapter translating application standard method to platform standard method. It will create a operation bean object with necessary information, such as class name

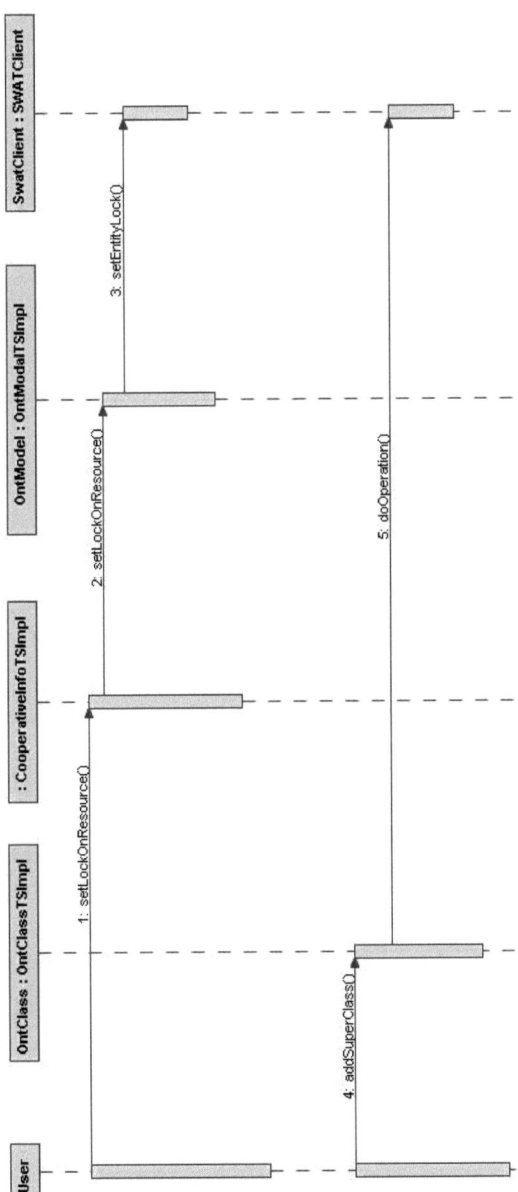

Figure 7.8: The Diagram of the First Phrase of the Cooperation Awareness

and operation type, invoking the *doOperation()* and enabling SWAT platform to complete the modification procedure.

5. **doOperation()** method: It is a method offered by SWAT client. All modification functions, such as renaming the ontology resource, changing super class of the current class, setting domain area of the given ontology property, are proposed by triggering *doOperation()* method through different operation beans. This method will modify the data stored on the server side data storage. A group-awareness event will be distributed to all participated clients after modification is done.

After one user sets lock on the given ontology resource, the SWAT platform will add a new command in the session space controlling the multi-user actions. It generates a locking event and distributes it to all other clients so that they get awareness of locking procedure. Fig 7.9 indicates the process sequence of this phase. In this phase we used Java listener pattern to receive event notification.

1. **processLockEvent()** method: When someone sets a lock on a given resource, the SWAT platform generates a locking event and distributes it to all interesting clients who are already registered for getting awareness. The event contains information of locks, such as who set the lock and which resource was locked.

2. **fireCooperativePrograss()** method: The *AwareComponentImpl* object is a realization of the interface of *AwareComponent* by means of receiving event notification from the SWAT platform. The method will be triggered once it receives a lock event. While the editor application can not understand the event format of the SWAT platform, event information will be retrieved and delivered to the *OntModelTSImpl* object through *fireCooperativePrograss* method.

3. **cooperativeOperationHappend()** method: The *CooperativeEventHandler* is the listener for receiving event notifications. Cooperative event, such as locking event and chatting event, will be delivered to the listeners through this method.

4. **fireCooperativeLockEvent()** method: All cooperation events will be delivered though the *cooperativeOperationHappend* method. The listener of *CooperativeEventHandler* will analysis the event type and fire the corresponding event delivering method.

5. **lockEventHappend()** method: The *CooperativeInfoTSImpl* executes the *CooperativeInfo* interface. This object generates the standard application event type and handles certain calculation-related event, such as finding out the proper position of the given ontology class in the class taxonomy tree structure. *CooperativeDecorateListener* is the listener interface operated by GUI objects with the view to get notifications. For example, the class editor GUI employs this listener to obtain notification and displays a lock icon on the tree to users.

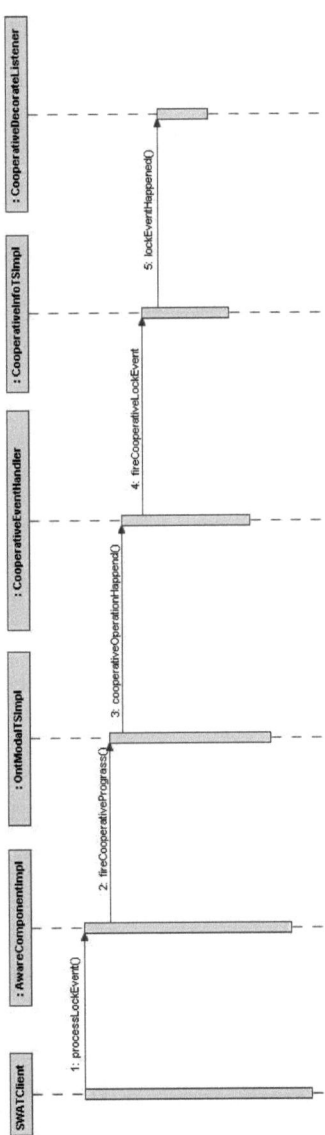

Figure 7.9: The Sequence of Receiving Notifications and Process Them for Supporting the Cooperation Awareness

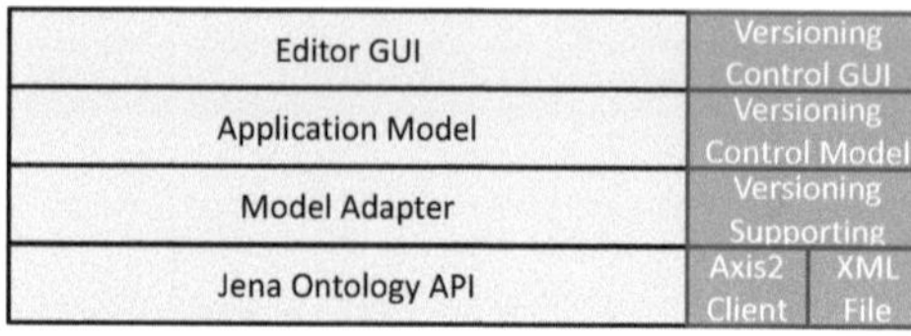

92

Editor GUI	Versioning Control GUI
Application Model	Versioning Control Model
Model Adapter	Versioning Supporting
Jena Ontology API	Axis2 Client / XML File

Figure 7.10: The Architecture of the Application on the Client Side

7.2 Versioning Support for Editors

While the Ontoverse editor, the first prototype implemented, provides important cooperation support functions such as awareness or locking, it is mainly focused on synchronous editing. Asynchronous styles of cooperation are less well supported. To address this issue, a subsequent second prototype development was focused on asynchronous cooperation in a distributed environment. In this environment the ontology will be divided into small units and each unit has a unique ID and a version number. A shared consensual ontology will be achieved by a set of actions synchronizing changed units, such as updating and committing.

The development of this environment is based on the Ontoverse editor. However, the implementation of the editor and the environment is quite much different from the original Ontoverse editor. In this section we will discuss about the implementation of the environment in details.

7.2.1 Architecture of the Versioning Support Environment.

The environment utilizes the client/server architecture. The application on the server side offers a set of methods to retrieve and save units so as to manage a repository for various clients. The application on the client side supports an API for different ontology editors. By launching this API the editors can easily connect to the repository and control unit version of an ontology.

The Fig 7.10 indicates the architecture of the system on the client side. On the client side, we employ an ontology editor based on the Ontoverse editor. As discussed in the previous section, we know that the Ontoverse editor occupies an intermediate layer between the editor model layer and the SWAT platform layer. By means of this layer we can switch the editor from SWAT platform to other ontology APIs or platforms. Under the versioning supporting environment, it is necessary to preserve the private version of the ontology on a private workspace, hence,in this case instead of SWAT platform we use Jena ontology API. Based on the Jena ontology API users are able to edit the ontology on their own workspace. The ontology file will be stored at different client sides. The version control system helps users reach their consensus of the ontology on a shared workspace and the system then acts as a plugin application to the ontology editor.

The plugin application is equipped with several layers as shown in the figure. The *GUI layer* displays the version control GUI for users. The GUI layer presents the changed units and can perform synchronous actions, such as updating the ontology units to private workspace that have been changed by other users. The *version control model* manages the data which are employed by GUI layer, such as all the units to be committed to the server. The *versioning supporting layer* is the key component in the system. This layer is entitled to accomplish two tasks. Firstly, it should manage the local client information, such as controlling the local changed status of the unit; the second task is to communicate with the server side system, compare and/or merge the local and repository units. It offers a standard API and can be used by any other ontology editors. The *axis2 client* is the component operated by the versioning supporting layer. It offers a set of methods for upper layer application to communicate with the server side system. This layer can be switched by other connection techniques, such as socket technique or CORBA technique. To control the version information of the ontology, it will be saved both on the client side and the repository(server) side. The *XML File* component helps the previous layer manage the version information on the client side. Currently, we employ a XML file storing the version information. It is, however, not mandatory. Besides the XML file, other mediums, such as plain text file or database is also applicable.

The server side system manages the data storage and provides a set of method to retrieve and save units. Fig 7.11 grants us an overview of the architecture of the server side system.

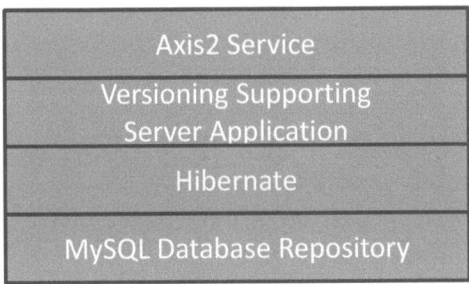

Figure 7.11: The Application Controlling the Versioning Repository on the Server Side

The *Axis2 Service layer* is the interface used by different clients. A number of methods have been provided, such as saving a unit to the repository. Since a repository space will be created to manage an ontology file or project, it offers several methods to manage the project, such as creating a new repository space. The *Versioning Supporting Server Application* is the main application running on the server side. It receives the client requirements, processes them, communicates with the database, performs the proper calculations, and finally returns the answers back. The *MySQL Database* is the place where all information are saved. The application of the *Hibernate* platform realizes the possibility of employing different database systems.

7.2.2   The Classes Used in the System

To control versioning for ontologies, there are three major tasks for our system, as follows:

1. dividing the ontology into fine-grained level of units. At the client side ontology will be synchronized with the one saved on the shared workspace by synchronizing these ontology units. Only the changed part of the ontology will be synchronized so that modification information can be preserved and version can be controlled on the level of ontology resources.

2. managing the units storage on the server. The repository is the shared workspace for all ontology developers. Through performing certain actions, such as committing, merging or updating, consensus will be got among different users, thus the system should be able to save and retrieve the units from the repository and manage the possible conflicts among users.

3. offering a set of methods for ontology editors so that they can easily build a plugin application to manage version of ontologies. Important functions, such as how to merge the different units, or how to get the unit from the repository, will be wrapped and editor programmers do not need to know detailed methodologies to support such functions.

Such task decomposition leads to three main packages of the Java classes accordingly. A shared package of Java classes to be used by both client and server side applications defines how to manage ontology units in the Java environment. A client package offers a standard API for ontology editors, and a server package controls the data storage on the server side.

Fig 7.12 demonstrates the class definition of the shared package. As discussed in the chapter 6 we will employ the definition of CBD to limit the scope of an ontology resource. There are several basic elements which were adopted to implement the methodology:

- **Label**. An ontology can be seen as a set of triples. Each of them is represented as a *String*. The string is a URI, which delegates an ontology resource, or a URI with value, which denotes a literal. To denote a literal, the string takes a format of 'URI@Value'. The *URI* part of the string defines the type of the literal and the *Value* part indicates the value of the literal. The class *Label* is thus employed to represent this string object. Several methods in the class serve to save or set the string object. In the system we allocate each ontology resource with an ID so that they can be traced after renamed. Such ID will be stored in the class.

- **RDFNode**. The *Label* class is the composition of the *RDFNode* class, with certain methods that can determine if the current node is an ontology resource or a literal.

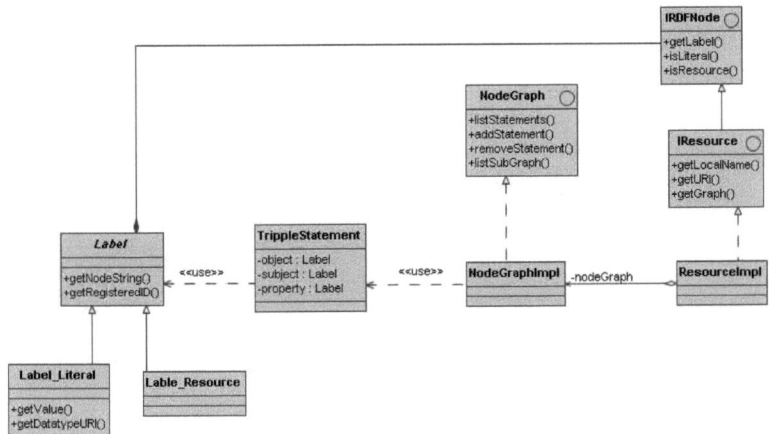

Figure 7.12: Class Diagram of the Shared Package

- **IResource/ResourceImpl.** The smallest unit to control version of an ontology is the ontology resource. The Java interface of *IResource* and its implementation *ResourceImpl* are used to denote the definition of ontology resource in the Java environment. It is the sub-class of the *RDFNode* class and enjoys several methods to access the ontology resource data. For example the *getLocalName()* method returns the local name of the ontology resource. The *ResourceImpl* class contains a set of triples indicating the CBD area of the resource.

- **NodeGraph/NodeGraphImpl.** The CBD area of an ontology resource contains a set of triples. Chapter 6 has defined the scope of the triples and the method how to obtain these triples. The interface *NodeGraph* and its implmentation *NodeGraphImpl* class are employed to manage these triples. A set of methods were developed to support saving and retrieving of the triples. We also developed certain methods that can list sub-graphs of the current CBD graph. They will put into force when the ontology resource contains anonymous resources. The *NodeGraphImpl* Java class is the composition of the *ResourceImpl* Java class.

- **TripleStatment.** The triples in the *NodeGraphImpl* are represented in the *TrippleStatment* classes where subject, object and property are stored. Their attributes are *Label* class and hence can either be an ontology resource or a literal.

The shared package can be applied both at the server side and the client side. The versioning system controls the development process of the ontology development. Users commit their changes to the server side and retrieve the collaborative change by other users from the server and update their local copy of the ontology.

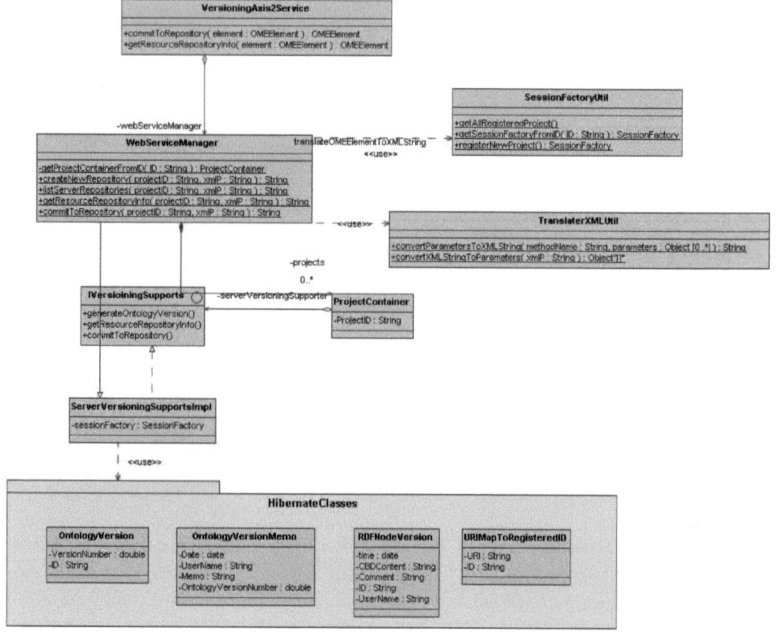

Figure 7.13: Class Diagram for the Server Side Application

Meanwhile, the server side application is responsible for data management and employs a database to store the information of ontology resources. Fig 7.13 reveals the class definitions at the server side.

- **VersioningAxis2Service**. The VersioningAxis2Service is the service interface designed to use Axis2 platform. Client applications connect to the Axis2 Web Service and send request to it. The interface defines all the methods that client applications need. For example, by means of *commitToRepository()* the client application will save their ontology resources into the server database. The *getResourceRepositoryInfo()* method returns the resource's CBD area of the given URL with its version information, such as who and when it committed. To invoke these methods, client applications need to identify which ontology project they would adopt with the project ID. The parameters deployed in this class are all *DOMElement* objects. The service will get parameters carried by the DOMElement and transfer them to the next class. It is a delegation of the *IVersioningSupports* interface in the Axis2 environment.

- **WebServiceManager**. To increase the feasibility and the robustness of the system, we developed this class to manage the request and this class isolates the detailed information of the service while parameters are all in string format. It is a static class so that it can be operated by several classes simultaneously and thereby controls the synchronization in the multi-user environment. As we will see later that one *Server VersioningSupportsImpl* object manages a database connection and serves for clients as an ontology project service provider, this class also manages the *Server VersioningSupportsImpl* objects. When requests from the client side in need of an ontology project service provider, this class will search out the proper provider based on the project ID passed from the client application and then delivers the requests to it. If necessary it will create new provider object in case that no such instance was created before. Since the computer resource will be consumed by running the database constantly, this class will be released after a period without receiving further requests.

- **IVersioningSupports/ServerVersioningSupportsImpl.** The *IVersioningSupports* interface defines the service employed by client applications. In this class we utilize standard Java objects, such as String, double, int, etc. The implmentation class *Server VersioningSupportsImpl* activates the interface and offers the access to requests, such as drawing information from the database. Hence, it is a service provider, and each instance deals with one database connection, providing service for one ontology project.

- **HibernateClasses.** They are set of classes employed by the *Hibernate* platform. The Hibernate platform enables us to utilize various databases without modifying the source code of the application. Each class delegates a database table.

- **TranslaterXMLUtil.** As discussed before, the parameters employed in the Axis2 platform are OEMElement format whereas the logical processing disposes of standard Java data format. In order to support different connection platforms we serialized all parameters into XML document and afterwards into string format manually. This class offers methods of translating Java standard parameters into XML document or vice versa.

The client application gives ontology editors an API so that they can build private ontology controlling system accordingly. The API offers a set of easy-for-using methods and it is responsible for the connection to the repository. Fig 7.14 illustrates the class diagram.

We will hereby describe some important classes and the functions:

- **IVersioningAssistor/VersioningAssistorIForJenaXML.** We use the IVersioningAssistor interface to identify a set of methods to be employed by ontology editor developers. These methods support to build an Plug-in application for controlling version for ontologies. These methods include:

  1. *initVersioningForResource().* Once the method is triggered, the system will find out all named resources, and will obtain a unique ID from the server in the scope of the current project. The assigned ID with the URI of the ontology resource will then be saved into a local space. Currently

98

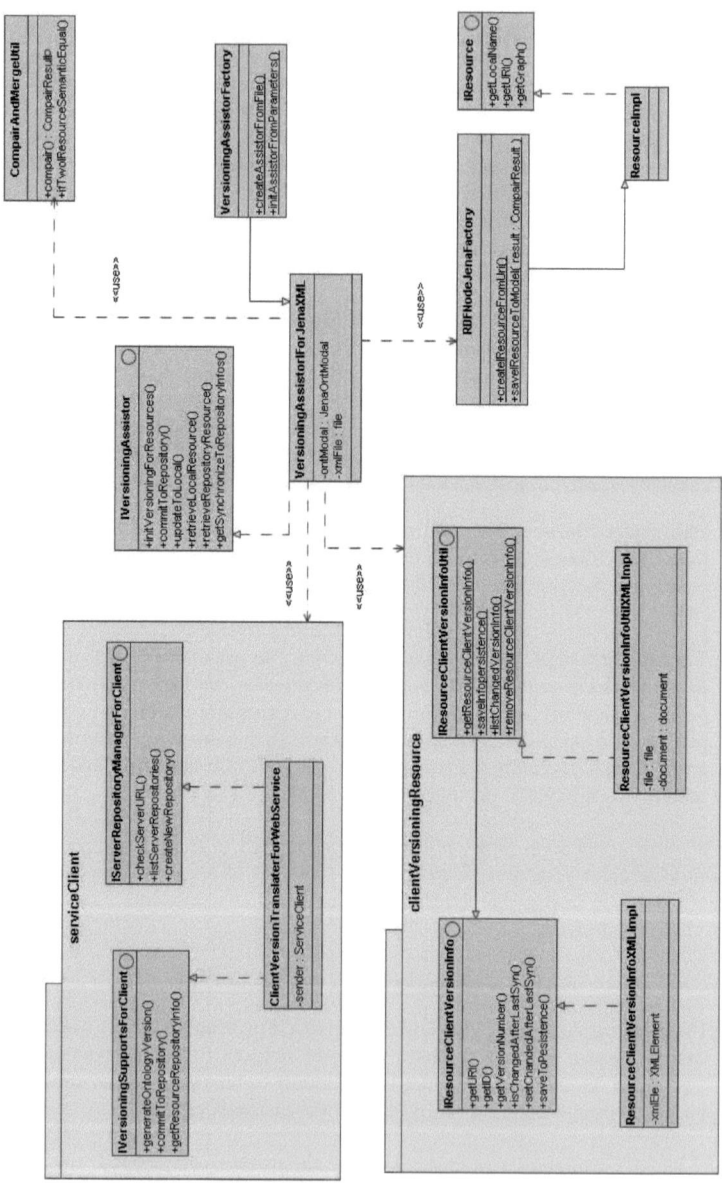

Figure 7.14: Class Diagram of the Client Application

we will save them into a XML file in the same directory with the ontology file. Once the version information is initialized, the system can then trace the editing change for each named ontology resource.

2. *getSynchronizeToRepositoryInfos()*. The system will accomplish a synchronization check once invoked. The system will firstly check if any local changes have been performed and enlist all changed resource marked as 'NeedToCommit'. The resources, that have been changed by collaborative users, will also be found out by marking with 'NeedToUpdate'. Once a resource has both the states of 'NeedToCommit' and 'NeedToUpdate' ,it implies a conflict inside it. The return value of the method is a list containing resources to be synchronized with the repository.

3. *updateToLocal()*. The system will update the ontology resource in the local copy of the ontology given the *IResource* information from the repository. Local versioning information will also be updated.

4. *commitToRepository()*. Similar to the local resource updating method, this method will transfer the *IResource* retrieved from local ontology file to the repository. Versioning information stored on the repository side will also be changed.

Some detailed discussions of these methods will be further stated in the next sub-section. Since the distributed Ontoverse editor relies on Jena ontology API, we implemented a class supporting Jena OntModel ontology model. This *VersioningAssistorlForJenaXML* class employs XML file to save versioning information at the local side.

• **RDFNodeJenaFactory**. As we used *IResource* of the shared package to represent the smallest unit in version controlling, it is necessary to capture ontology resource information from the Jena ontology API and generate the corresponding IResource object. In addition, We also need to save the IResource object into the Jena model. Such translation can be performed by this class.

• **CompairAndMergeUtil**. A significant function by versioning control systems is that it could tell if two ontology resources are different and where the difference lies. This class provides several methods in distinguishing different *IResource* objects. In case of discrepancy, the class will enlist the different *triplestatements*. Updating of local ontology file is also based on the result.

• **serviceClient**. This package includes several classes responsible for the management of connection with the repository. The architecture is quite similar to the one on the server side.

• **clientVersioningResource**. This package deals with the representation of local versioning information and its storage. Local versioning information will be wrapped into the *IResourceClientVersionInfo*, which defines the necessary functions for the system, once it accesses the versioning information on the client side. For example, the *isChangedAfterLasySyn()* method will be employed in synchronization in order to find out which ontology resources have been changed. In this way, each named ontology resource has a corresponding object of *IResourceClientVersionInfo*. The *IResourceClientVersionInfoUtil* interface defines a set of methods to operate such objects.

7.2.3 Detailed Discussion of Some Important Procedures

The previous sub-section indicates that by way of the class diagram the system can be implemented both on client and server side. Seen from the system architecture, the increased software layers improve the feasibility of the system. However, it also leads to system complexity that refrains from comprehension. In this section we will demonstrate a detailed introduction of how we implemented the system.

How to Invoke the Service from the Client Application?

The invocation of service may access several classes and interfaces, under the principle that the system to be built is independent of any concrete platforms. Fig 7.15 illustrates the sequence diagram of how to call the service. The procedure is presented as the following figure 7.15:

1. *commitToRepository()*. The *IVersioningAssistor* provides the API with upper layer software components, which are normally the models operated by different ontology editors. To implement the interface, it is essential to employ commitToRepository() method offered by the interface *IVersioningSupportsForClient* which commits local resource to the repository. The parameters of the method are standard Java classes.

2. *send()*. The implementation of the *IVersioningSupportsForClient* receives the invocation from the *IVersioningAssistor* and serializes the parameters into string format. The serialization employs a XML document as medium, where the values of parameters will be written with their class types so that a string will then be generated. The *send()* method offered by the Axis2 platform sends information to the repository side. We set the serialized string parameters to the *OMEElement* class and send it to the Axis2 platform.

3. *commitToRepository(OMEElement=)*. The *VersioningAxis2Service* receives the *OMEElement* objects and get the serialized parameter from it. The class will deliver the string parameter to the *WebServiceManager* class.

4. *commitToRepository(...)*. The parameters of all methods in the class *WebServiceManager* are the same. The first parameter indicates to which project the method invocation belongs . The second parameter is the serialized XML document containing necessary parameters to trigger the service. The *WebServiceManager* will find out the proper *IVersioningSupports* as a service provider, who delivers the service invocation with standard Java parameters unserialized from the input string formatted parameters.

101

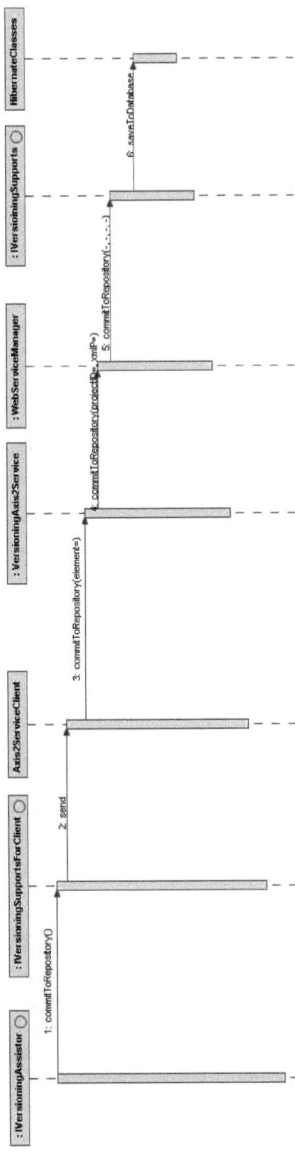

Figure 7.15: The diagram illustrates how to invoke the service from the client side

5. *saveToDatabase*. The implementation of *IVersioningSupports* returns the proper result to the client applications. By means of the *Hibernate* platform, data will be saved and retrieved from the database.

Judging from the above arguments, different distribution platforms can be employed, since all Java standard parameters will be serialized into a string format.

Identifying Changes before Synchronization?

When a user intends to synchronize his local copy of ontology to the repository, the first step is to find out which resources need be synchronized. This will be calculated by the system API. Fig 7.16 presents the sequence diagram of this procedure.

1. *startSynchronization()*. To commit a change to the repository and update the collaborative changes into the local copy, the user needs to firstly find out those resources to be synchronized. Usually by clicking a button, such procedure will be triggered.

2. *getSynchronizeToRepositoryInfos()*. Through the method offered by the system API, the application model could enlist all named resources to be synchronized.

3. *listChangedVersionInfo()* and *getResourceRepositoryInfo()*. Two kinds of changes should be disclosed through such searching method. Firstly, it should find out what the user has changed in his local copy of the ontology and commit the changes to the repository. Moreover, it should also find out the resources which are changed by other users. To track such collaborative changes, some methods provided by the service play an important role. For example, the method of *getResourceRepositoryInfo()* will retrieve the latest server side information of a given resource URI, which is a important function for the whole procedure. Fig 7.17 demonstrates the flow diagram of it.

4. *sendRequest*. The system follows the sequence introduced in 7.2.3 to get proper results from the repository side.

How to Perform Synchronization?

When all changed resources, including local changes and collaborative changes, are listed out, the system will perform synchronization based on the state of the changes. If a resource is changed by the local user, the system will commit it to the repository, obtain the latest version number and perform local update. If a resource is changed by the collaborative users, the system will receive the server copy and merge it to the local one. Meanwhile, the local version information will be updated. The flow diagram of Fig. 7.18 illustrates the procedure.

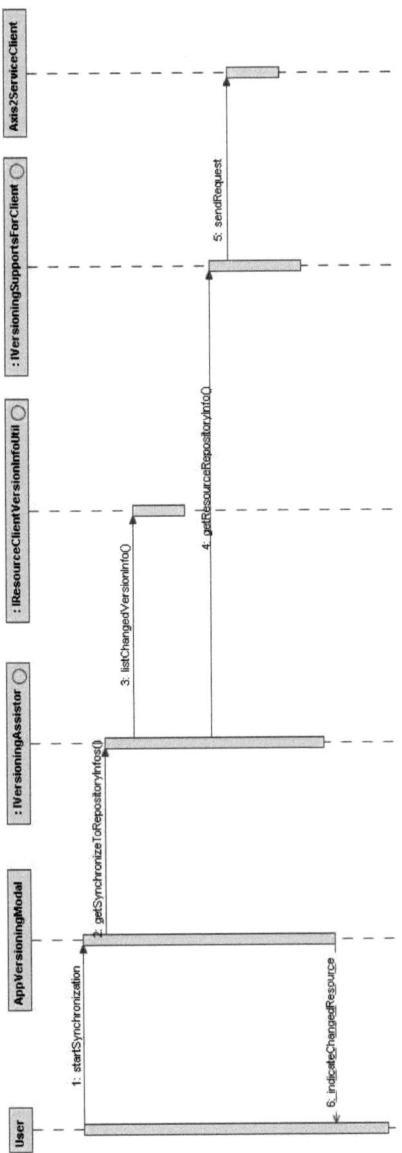

Figure 7.16: The Sequence Diagram of Finding Changed Resources

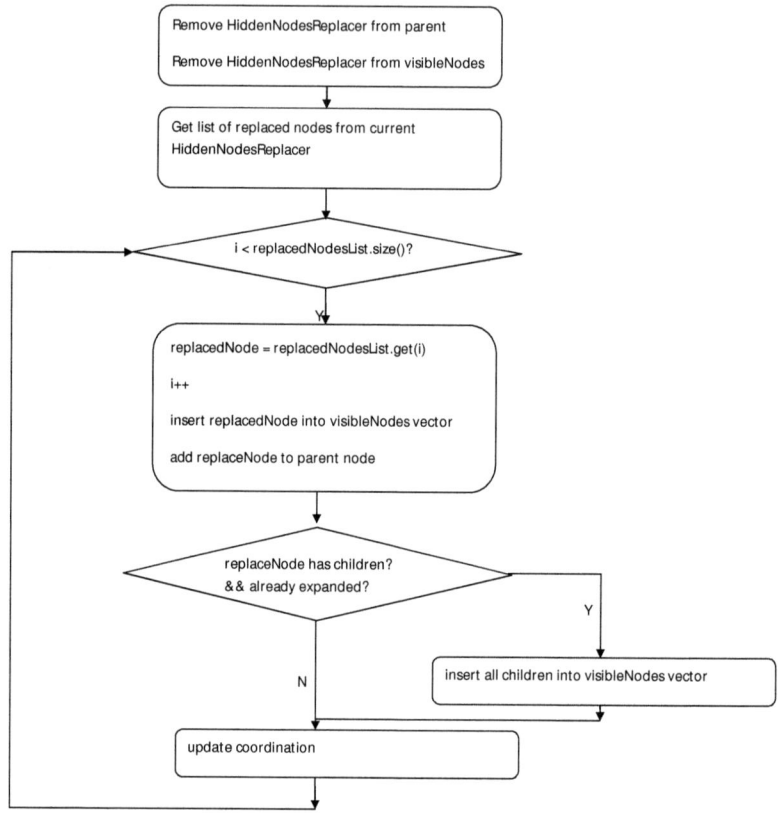

Figure 7.17: Flow Diagram of Finding Changed Resources

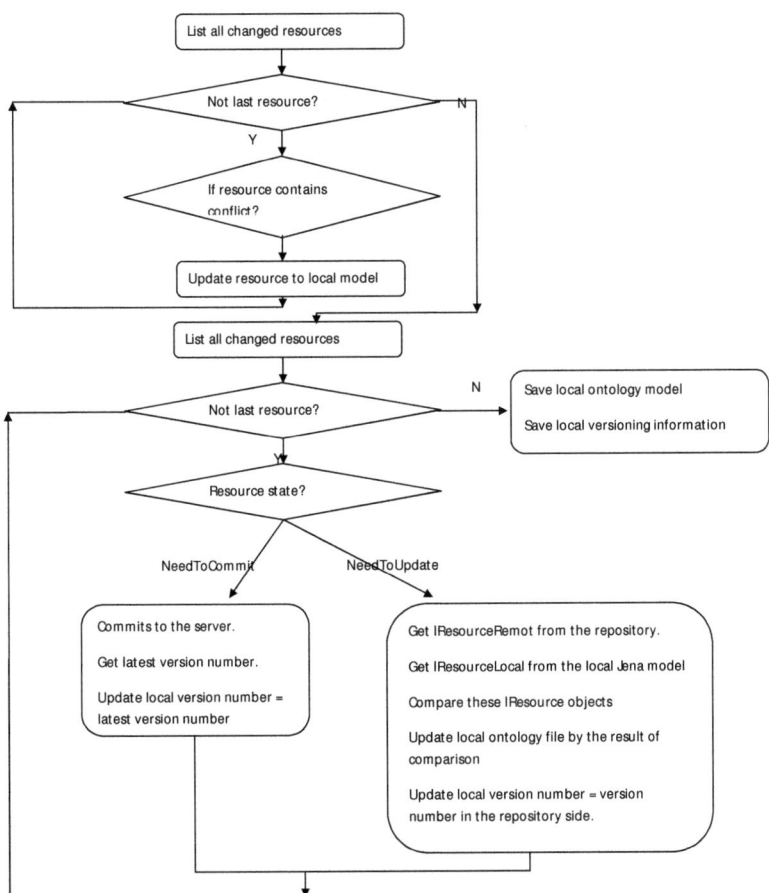

Figure 7.18: Making Synchronization by Commiting or Updating Changes

Chapter 8

Evaluation and Conclusions

In this thesis we have presented methods and two prototype systems for supporting ontology development in a collaborative environment. We first introduced the
methodologies and tools currently used in supporting collaborative ontology development. Several relevant requirements were elaborated based on analyzing the
shortcomings of current tools. We have developed two editors implementing those
requirements. In this chapter we will evaluate what we learned from the version
control system used to support collaborative ontology development in a distributed
environment and draw our conclusions.

8.1 Initial Evaluation of the Version Control Sys-
tem

To perform an initial qualitative evaluation, the version control system was used in
the early stages of producing an ontology for the subject areas of Human–Computer
Interaction (HCI). The HCI ontology is intended both for teaching purposes and for
subsequent indexing of research literature from the field. A small specialist group
from our lab was chartered to construct such an ontology. The group was composed
of one senior researcher, two doctoral students, and two masters students, all with
a background in this field and some general or specialized knowledge. To evaluate
the method and the system, the users were asked to build the ontology using our
system. All participants worked in separate offices and installed the single user editor locally. The evaluation phase lasted for two weeks.

A prototype ontology was created by one participant (a doctoral student) in the
first step. After he committed it to the shared repository, the other participants
downloaded it and stored it locally through our plug-in versioning system. After
one week's trial operation, 17 classes were added to the prototype ontology while
8 classes were altered. The maximal change happened in ontology class *Human*, it
went from Rv1.0 to Rv4.0 by four users. Fig. 6.7 shows a fragment of this result.

A review session was organized after the first week. In this session the users were asked to provide feedback on the system and the process. There was generally a positive feedback about the synchronization features provided. The different views embedded in the editors which clearly exposed the versioning mechanism led to an intensive discussion both of top-level and lower level concepts. While the concrete editing process using versioning was considered to be very supportive, users also expressed a wish to support the early phase in a more extensive way where major structural changes are likely to happen. These changes were somewhat hard to follow even when history information was provided. A need for more informal and less structured collaboration support, synchronous and asychnronous, was articulated although such functions were outside the scope of the current system.

The versioning support appeared to be more useful in the later stages, where smaller changes happened such as adding new subclasses or renaming a resource. However, it is evident that a longer evaluation phase will be needed to assess the tool's value in later stages of the development. Some users pointed out the differences between software development and ontology development. Though the system offers similar functionalities as systems, such as CVS or SVN, for ontology version controlling, it does not supply very much assistance for users' collaboration in the first ontology development phase. Different from software implementation, where every class may contain hundreds of lines of code, the description of an ontology resource is much more concise, especially at the beginning stage of development. Modifications during the early phase are mainly related to changes of structure, such as changing the parent of a class which is often associated with a name change. The content of an ontology resource, such as its annotation information or links to other resources, are typically ignored at this stage. The participants of the study, however, expressed the view that when the basic structure of the ontology is stable and work begins to focus on, for instance, extracting concept definitions from documents, the system would be very helpful and would support the collaboration .

The increased error tolerance of modifications was also mentioned. Since every step can be traced later from the system, users felt more freedom to make modifications regardless of the absolute correctness of the change. One could speculate that this feature can motivate users to become more engaged in the process although our results cannot yet corroborate this. More support for ontology comparison was also demanded for the initial phases. Some users would like to develop more complete individual versions before exchanging and comparing them with the proposals of other users. Furthermore, some users underlined the importance of being able to provide and see comments explaining the rationale of the currently submitted versions, yet this feature was hardly used. It is still an open issue how users could be motivated to provide more explanations for their actions.

8.2 Conclusions and Future Work

The aim of this work was to improve collaborative ontology development and try to answer open research questions related to supporting such cooperation during the development process. After introducing the current development methodologies and some popular editors, we concluded that there are several general requirements when developers want to build an ontology collaboratively. Among these requirements, the request for social support, private workspaces, as well as version control during development, are missing from almost all current ontology development editors.

To cope with the requirement of social support, some mature existing techniques can be used or seen as good references. The newly emerged social networks provide users with a platform, bringing friends to people, and grouping them into a virtual community. The relationship of people is closer and the way of communication is enriched. The advantage offered by such a technique was demanded for the ontology editors by the community of ontology developers. Discussion forums, profiles of users, and wikis are common social techniques. These techniques can also help ontology developers work in a close environment. We have applied these techniques in the Ontoverse platform. Ontology developers join in a virtual society in this platform and use techniques, such as wiki and paper repository, to communicate with each other asynchronously and manage original resources used in building ontologies. The Java-applet based ontology editor works closely with the wiki-based web platform. Some documents, such as requirement documents and ontology specifications, can be accessed at any time by the involved users. End users can also use forum to propose their suggestions or additional requirements during their usage of the ontologies. These information helps developers optimize their products. The repository helps developers extract concept names from knowledge bases and it also manages the knowledge resources for the ontology.

While a number of collaborative ontology editors are capable of providing some level of group-awareness among developers, they usually support only a single shared workspace for a group of developers. The lack of providing private workspace means that the private view of a domain concept can not be preserved during the process of development. One of the possible advantages offered by collaborative development is that multiple aspects of thinking for one concept may increase the veracity of the definitions. Without private workspace, however, developer's private points of view of a concept may be easily ignored or overlapped by other users. Many collaborative environments with cooperation supporting complex tasks offer private workspace for users, a programming editor is one example. It is almost impossible for programmers to code without private workspace for their work. The prototype of ontology version control system offers private workspace for each user. Developers work asynchronously or even off-line in such an environment. Personal aspects of domain concepts will be well conserved and conflicts are very noticeable during synchronization, if a proper methodology of dealing with these conflicts is chosen, an accurate definition of the concept may be reached.

None of the current editors manage versions on the level of ontology resources. Some platforms control the version on the level of the entire ontology file. The change of such version number indicates that the ontology has been changed, but it can not tell users, e.g., how many ontology resources have been changed and who performed such changes. Controlling versions on ontology resources provides a history of the modifications for a concept. Moreover, a distribution of an ontology contains not only the ontology resources but also their individual version information. The applications may be updated to cope with the latest version ontologies by analyzing this resource version information. The version number of the ontology could be also used to indicate differences between versions. The number of the version may indicate the type of change, for example a backward compatible change may increase only the decimal part of the version number. The prototype ontology version control system developed provides a solution to these problems. In this system, the version of each concept in the ontology is controlled. Modifications performed on an ontology resource, for example an ontology class, will be preserved and the list of changes for that concept can be traced later. The version of the ontology contains the list of versions of all involved ontology resources.

Though the current systems give us an environment in which to build ontologies, a number of optimization and reinforcements need to be implemented. The solution to support more effective group-awareness needs to be considered, and the continued development of the current version control system is also demanded.

8.2.1 A Suggestion in Providing Better Group-awareness

Supporting group-awareness is one of basic functions supported by most of current ontology development environments. However, it is still worthy of studying the mechanism to implement such function because of low effective that many tools currently have. In using them users are likely to either ignore important awarenesses or never get them.

What kinds of awareness are important to the users involved? Should the system (sender) deliver all events to other users? Or should the receiver require the change events that he is interested in? How to define "interesting" events? Personal work may be interrupted if too many less-important awarenesses have been received. On the other hand, important events may be ignored if too few awarenesses have been delivered. During the development of the editors, we may find a solution for choosing the appropriate awareness.

Conflicts may take place when a number of developers are working on the same part of an ontology. In the version control system conflicts means that multiple developers are working on the same ontology resources. Once the conflicts occur, developers need to solve the conflicts before they merge their working copy into the repository. A proper method used to solve the conflicts increases the result quality. For example, a discussion between two developers helps them find a better solution for defining a concept in the ontology when a conflict occurs. In the first prototype editor and many current editors, which use only one shared workspace and use a lock mechanism to control the editing sequence, conflicts may be easily ignored. For example, the second user will simply remove some triples of the ontology class and add new triples based on his own opinion, while the removed triples are the opinion of the first develop and thus the personal view of the first developer is lost. Such conflicts should be explicitly noticeable for involved developers.

We extend the definition of conflict during the development of ontologies: a conflicts may occur if there is a *collision range* among the users' knowledge base. Fig. 8.1 indicates the collision range of co-workers. The left cycle indicates the knowledge base of the user "Tim" and the right one indicates the knowledge base of the user "Lang." The overlapped area means the *collision range* of the multiple users' knowledge base in which they have their own opinion for certain concepts. While the features and attributes of the concept are objective, the knowledge of the concept is subjective. It is difficult for one person to confirm that his knowledge and cognition of a concept is correct. However, the definition of such concepts may be more objective when several users give their own interpretations and try to reach a consensus by means of discussion and debate. Only the collaborative work performed within the collision range helps people optimize their definition of the concept. Collaborative work does not help much if a single user is doing his job in the non-collision area.

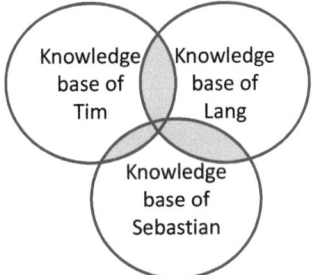

Figure 8.1: The Conflict Area of Multiple Users

From the discussion above we can conclude that not all collaborative events are necessary for each user, but only those events which are within the possible collision range of the users (the shadow area of Fig. 8.1) should be acknowledged. The user should not be aware of the other events, for example Lang should not receive the events which relate to the collision range of users "Tim" and "Sebastian."

Though the knowledge bases of the co-workers define the range of collision, different applications use different strategies to decide the boundary of the possible collision range. In the ontology editor, a simple definition of the collision range could be based on maintaining lists of all resources changed by the different users and resources depending on them. For example if the ontology resource, which has been changed by a user, is modified by other users, it is a conflict relating to the user's knowledge base and the system should explicitly remind him of the occurrence of such a conflict. If a user created a new ontology class and set it as the child class of one ontology class, which the user has modified some days before, the editor should remind him in a relative weak mode.

Based on this theory we suggest providing a method which determines how strong the conflicts are. The higher the value it returns, the stronger the collision is. If the value is quite high, which happens in our scenario when other users changed the resources that the current user changed before, the system usually needs to indicate such conflict in a explicit way, for example indicates a flash icon beside the resource in the taxonomy tree to help the user notice the modification. If the value is medium the system may display it in the status bar of the editor window so that it can be revealed without interrupting the current job. The system may not display anything if the value is very low or zero because it is irrelevant with the user.

With the help of this method, we can understand which awareness events should be received by involved users and in which way the system should display such events. We could implement the group-awareness function in the future application based on this method.

8.2.2 Future Work of Ontology Version-Control-System

Currently there are two editors offering different aspects of collaborative support, one is based on a shared workspace and offers group-awareness for participating developers, another is based on the version control system and controls the version at the level of the ontology resources. However, it is possible to merge these two approaches. The provision of private workspaces does in principle not preclude for offering group-awareness. Though the second prototype does not demand on-line working during editing, the broad existence of networks can be used to support group-awareness. We developed an event subscribe/publish mechanism among the axis2 platform[4]. With the help of this mechanism collaborative events, such as change events and user login events, can be delivered to client applications through the axis2 platform. Synchronous event notification can thus be implemented in the version control system.

Since we control versions on the level of ontology resources, it is possible to give developers the ability to *roll back* their modification of a ontology resource to its previous version. Challenges are that we need to analyze whether such a rollback can be performed and how to roll back such resources without destroying the consistency of the entire ontology.

We may give specific and informative meanings to the parts of the version number. For example, the change in the decimal part indicates that this change does not alter the semantic meaning of the ontology resource. Thus end users could easily decide whether they should update their application as well.

Bibliography

[1] Grigoris Antoniou and Frank van Harmelen. *A Semantic Web Primer.* MIT Press, Cambridge, MA, 2. edition, 2008.

[2] Sören Auer, Sebastian Dietzold, , Thomas Riechert, and Thomas Riechert. Ontowiki - a tool for social, semantic collaboration. In *The Semantic Web - ISWC 2006, 5th International Semantic Web Conference, ISWC 2006,* pages 736–749. Springer, 2006.

[3] Ronald M. Baecker, Jonathan Grudin, William Buxton, and Saul Greenberg. *Readings in Human-Computer Interaction: Toward the Year 2000.* Morgan Kaufmann, January 1995.

[4] Fan Bai and Wang Tao. Message broker using asynchronous method invocation in web service and its evaluation. *Software Testing Verification and Validation Workshop, IEEE International Conference on,* 0:265–273, 2010.

[5] Victor R. Basili and Albert J. Turner. Iterative enhancement: A practical technique for software development. *IEEE Trans. Software Eng.,* 1(4):390–396, 1975.

[6] Sean Bechhofer, Ian Horrocks, Carole Goble, and Robert Stevens. Oiled: A reason-able ontology editor for the semantic web. In Franz Baader, Gerhard Brewka, and Thomas Eiter, editors, *KI 2001: Advances in Artificial Intelligence,* volume 2174 of *Lecture Notes in Computer Science,* pages 396–408. Springer Berlin / Heidelberg, 2001. 10.1007/3-540-45422-5_28.

[7] A. Bernaras, I. Laresgoiti, and J. Corera. Building and reusing ontologies for electrical network applications. In Wolfgang Wahlster, editor, *Proceedings of the 12th European Conference on Artificial Intelligence (ECAI 96): Budapest, Hungary: August 11-16,* pages 298–302. Wiley, 1996.

[8] Gilles Bisson. Why and how to define a similarity measure for object based representation systems. In *TOWARDS VERY LARGE KNOWLEDGE BASES,* pages 236–246. IOS Press, 1995.

[9] Guus Schreiber Bob, Bob Wielinga, and Wouter Jansweijer. The kactus view on the 'o' word. In *In IJCAI Workshop on Basic Ontological Issues in Knowledge Sharing,* pages 159–168, 1995.

[10] Willem Nico Borst. *Construction of Engineering Ontologies for Knowledge Sharing and Reuse.* PhD thesis, Enschede, September 1997.

116

[11] E. Bozsak, Marc Ehrig, Siegfried Handschuh, Andreas Hotho, Alexander Maedche, Boris Motik, Daniel Oberle, Christoph Schmitz, Steffen Staab, Ljiljana Stojanovic, Nenad Stojanovic, Rudi Studer, Gerd Stumme, York Sure, Julien Tane, Raphael Volz, and Valentin Zacharias. Kaon - towards a large scale semantic web. In Kurt Bauknecht, A. Min Tjoa, and Gerald Quirchmayr, editors, *E-Commerce and Web Technologies, Third International Conference, EC-Web 2002, Aix-en-Provence, France, September 2-6, 2002, Proceedings*, volume 2455 of *LNCS*, pages 304–313. Springer, 2002.

[12] Simone Braun, Andreas Schmidt, Andreas Walter, Gabor Nagypal, and Valentin Zacharias. Ontology maturing: a collaborative web 2.0 approach to ontology engineering. In Natasha Noy, Harith Alani, Gerd Stumme, Peter Mika, York Sure, and Denny Vrandecic, editors, *Proceedings of the Workshop on Social and Collaborative Construction of Structured Knowledge (CKC 2007) at the 16th International World Wide Web Conference (WWW2007) Banff, Canada, May 8, 2007*, volume 273 of *CEUR Workshop Proceedings*, 2007.

[13] Karin K. Breitman, Marco Antonio Casanova, and Walter Truszkowski. *Semantic Web: Concepts, Technologies and Applications*. NASA Monographs in Systems and Software Engineering. Springer, London, 2007.

[14] Jeremy J. Carroll. Signing rdf graphs. Technical Report HPL-2003-142, HP Labs, 2003.

[15] Jeremy J. Carroll and Jeremy J. Carroll. Signing rdf graphs. In *In 2nd ISWC*, volume 2870 of *LNCS*, pages 5–15. Springer, 2003.

[16] Oscar Corcho, Mariano Fernández-López, and Asunción Gómez-Pérez. Methodologies, tools and languages for building ontologies: where is their meeting point? *Data Knowl. Eng.*, 46:41–64, July 2003.

[17] Óscar Corcho, Mariano Fernández-López, Asunción Gómez-Pérez, and Óscar Vicente. Webode: An integrated workbench for ontology representation, reasoning, and exchange. In Asunción Gómez-Pérez and V. Benjamins, editors, *Knowledge Engineering and Knowledge Management: Ontologies and the Semantic Web*, volume 2473 of *Lecture Notes in Computer Science*, pages 295–310. Springer Berlin / Heidelberg, 2002. 10.1007/3-540-45810-7_16.

[18] J. Davies, D. Fensel, and F. vanHarmelen. Towards the semantic web: Ontology-driven knowledge management. Wiley, UK, 2003.

[19] Klaas Dellschaft, Hendrik Engelbrecht, Jos Monte Barreto, Sascha Rutenbeck, and Steffen Staab. Cicero: Tracking design rationale in collaborative ontology engineering. In *Proceedings of the ESWC 2008 Demo Session*, 2008.

[20] Y. Kitamura R. Mizoguchi E. Sunagawa, K. Kozaki. Management of dependency between two or more ontologies in an environment for distributed development. In *Proc. of the International Workshop on Semantic Web Foundations and Application Technologies (SWFAT2003)*, pages 35–41. Nara, 2003.

[21] Marc Ehrig. *Ontology Alignment: Bridging the Semantic Gap*, volume 4 of *Semantic Web And Beyond Computing for Human Experience*. Springer, 2007.

[22] Lee D. Erman, Frederick Hayes-Roth, Victor R. Lesser, and D. Raj Reddy. The Hearsay-II Speech-Understanding System: Integrating Knowledge to Resolve Uncertainty. *ACM Comput. Surv.*, 12(2):213–253, 1980.

[23] Adam Farquhar, Richard Fikes, and James Rice. The ontolingua server: a tool for collaborative ontology construction. In *International Journal of Human-Computer Studies*, 1996.

[24] Mariano Fernandez-Lopez, Asuncion Gomez-Perez, and Natalia Juristo. Methontology: from ontological art towards ontological engineering. In *Proceedings of the AAAI97 Spring Symposium*, pages 33–40, Stanford, USA, March 1997.

[25] T. Gabel, Y. Sure, and J. Voelker. Kaon ontology management infrastructure. Technical Report SEKT Deliverable D3.1.1.a, SEKT, 2004.

[26] John H. Gennari, Mark A. Musen, Ray W. Fergerson, William E. Grosso, Monica Crubzy, Henrik Eriksson, Natalya F. Noy, and Samson W. Tu. The evolution of protégé: An environment for knowledge-based systems development. *International Journal of Human-Computer Studies*, 58:89–123, 2002.

[27] Asuncion Gomez-Perez, Oscar Corcho-Garcia, and Mariano Fernandez-Lopez. *Ontological Engineering*. Springer-Verlag New York, Inc., Secaucus, NJ, USA, 2003.

[28] Asunción Gómez-Pérez, Natalia Juristo, and Juan Pazos. Evaluation and assessment of the knowledge sharing technology. In *Towards very large knowledge bases*, pages 289–296, Holanda, 1995. IOS Press.

[29] L. Gordon-Murnane. Social bookmarking, folksonomies, and web 2.0 tools. *Searcher Mag Database Prof*, 14(6):26–38, 2006.

[30] Thomas R. Gruber. A translation approach to portable ontology specifications. *Knowl. Acquis.*, 5:199–220, June 1993.

[31] M. Grüninger and M. Fox. Methodology for the Design and Evaluation of Ontologies. In *IJCAI'95, Workshop on Basic Ontological Issues in Knowledge Sharing, April 13, 1995*, 1995.

[32] C. W. Holsapple and K. D. Joshi. Description and analysis of existing knowledge management frameworks. In *Proceedings of the Thirty-Second Annual Hawaii International Conference on System Sciences- Volume 1 - Volume 1*, HICSS '99, pages 1072–, Washington, DC, USA, 1999. IEEE Computer Society.

[33] Clyde W. Holsapple and K. D. Joshi. A collaborative approach to ontology design. *Commun. ACM*, 45:42–47, February 2002.

118

[34] Robert Jaeschke, Andreas Hotho, Christoph Schmitz, and Gerd Stumme. Analysis of the publication sharing behaviour in BibSonomy. In U. Priss, S. Polovina, and R. Hill, editors, *Proceedings of the 15th International Conference on Conceptual Structures (ICCS 2007)*, volume 4604 of *Lecture Notes in Artificial Intelligence*, pages 283–295, Berlin, Heidelberg, July 2007. Springer-Verlag.

[35] Z.E. Jerroudi. *Eine interaktive Vorgehensweise für den Vergleich und die Integration von Ontologien.* Schriften zu Kooperations- und Mediensystemen. Josef Eul Verlag GmbH, 2010.

[36] M. Klein, D. Fensel, A. Kiryakov, and D. Ognyanov. Ontology versioning and change detection on the web. In *Proc. of the 13th European Conf. on Knowledge Engineering and Knowledge Management (EKAW02) (Siguenza, Spain)*, pages 197–212, 2002.

[37] Michael Klein and Natasha Noy. A component-based framework for ontology evolution. In *Proceedings of the Workshop on Ontologies and Distributed Systems, IJCAI 2003*, Acapulco, Mexico, August9, 2003.

[38] Konstantinos Kotis and A. Vouros. Human-centered ontology engineering: The hcome methodology. *Knowl. Inf. Syst.*, 10:109–131, July 2006.

[39] K. Kozaki, Y. Kitamura, M. Ikeda, and R. Mizoguchi. Development of an Environment for Building Ontologies Based on a Fundamental Consideration of Role and Relationship. *Transactions of the Japanese Society for Artificial Intelligence*, 17:196–208, 2002.

[40] Kouji Kozaki, Yoshinobu Kitamura, Mitsuru Ikeda, and Riichiro Mizoguchi. Hozo: An environment for building/using ontologies based on a fundamental consideration of role and relationship. In *Proc. of EKAW2002*, pages 213–218. Springer, 2002.

[41] Douglas B. Lenat and R. V. Guha. *Building Large Knowledge-Based Systems; Representation and Inference in the Cyc Project.* Addison-Wesley Longman Publishing Co., Inc., Boston, MA, USA, 1st edition, 1989.

[42] V. I. Levenshtein. Binary codes capable of correcting deletions, insertions and reversals. *Soviet Physics Doklady.*, 10(8):707–710, February 1966.

[43] Y. Li, Z. A. Bandar, and D. Mclean. An approach for measuring semantic similarity between words using multiple information sources. *Knowledge and Data Engineering, IEEE Transactions on*, 15(4):871–882, 2003.

[44] M.F. Lopez, A. Gomez-Perez, J.P. Sierra, and A.P. Sierra. Building a chemical ontology using methontology and the ontology design environment. *Intelligent Systems and their Applications, IEEE*, 14(1):37 –46, 1999.

[45] Nils Malzahn, Stefan Weinbrenner, Peter Hüsken, Jürgen Ziegler, and H. Ulrich Hoppe. Collaborative ontology development distributed architecture and visualization. 2007.

[46] S. Melnik, H. Garcia-Molina, and E. Rahm. Similarity flooding: a versatile graph matching algorithm and its application to schema matching. *Data Engineering, 2002. Proceedings. 18th International Conference on*, pages 117–128, 2002.

[47] Riichiro Mizoguchi, Mitsuru Ikeda, Kazuhisa Seta, and Johan Vanwelkenhuysen. Ontology for modeling the world from problem solving perspectives. In *Proc. of IJCAI-95 Workshop on Basic Ontological Issues in Knowledge Sharing*, pages 1–12, 1995.

[48] Christian Morbidoni, Giovanni Tummarello, Orri Erling, and Reto Bachmann-Gmuer. Rdfsync: efficient remote synchronization of rdf models. In Karl Aberer, Key-Sun Choi, Natasha Noy, Dean Allemang, Kyung-Il Lee, Lyndon J B Nixon, Jennifer Golbeck, Peter Mika, Diana Maynard, Guus Schreiber, and Philippe Cudre-Mauroux, editors, *Proceedings of the 6th International Semantic Web Conference and 2nd Asian Semantic Web Conference (ISWC/ASWC2007), Busan, South Korea*, volume 4825 of *LNCS*, pages 533–546, Berlin, Heidelberg, November 2007. Springer Verlag.

[49] Robert Neches, Richard Fikes, Tim Finin, Tom Gruber, Ramesh Patil, Ted Senator, and William R. Swartout. Enabling technology for knowledge sharing. *AI Mag.*, 12(3):36–56, 1991.

[50] Natalya F. Noy, Abhita Chugh, and Harith Alani. The ckc challenge: Exploring tools for collaborative knowledge construction. *IEEE Intelligent Systems*, 23(1), 2008.

[51] Natalya F. Noy, Abhita Chugh, William Liu, and Mark A. Musen. *A Framework for Ontology Evolution in Collaborative Environments*. 2006.

[52] Natalya F. Noy and Mark A. Musen. Promptdiff: a fixed-point algorithm for comparing ontology versions. In *Eighteenth national conference on Artificial intelligence*, pages 744–750, Menlo Park, CA, USA, 2002. American Association for Artificial Intelligence.

[53] Natalya Fridman Noy, Ray W. Fergerson, and Mark A. Musen. The knowledge model of protg-2000: Combining interoperability and flexibility. In Rose Dieng and Olivier Corby, editors, *EKAW*, volume 1937 of *Lecture Notes in Computer Science*, pages 17–32. Springer, 2000.

[54] Daniel E. O'Leary. Using ai in knowledge management: Knowledge bases and ontologies. *IEEE Intelligent Systems*, 13:34–39, May 1998.

[55] Tim O'Reilly. What is web 2.0. design patterns and business models for the next generation of software. http://www.oreillynet.com/pub/a/oreilly/tim/news/2005/09/30/what-is-web-20.html, September 2005. Stand 12.5.2009.

[56] Nokia Patrick Stickler. Cbd - concise bounded description. W3C member submission, retrieved from http://www.w3.org/Submission/CBD/, 2005.

[57] Ingo Paulsen, Katrin Weller Dominic Mainz, Jochen Kohl Indra Mainz, and Arndt Von Haeseler. Ontoverse: Collaborative ontology engineering for the life sciences. *Information - Wissenschaft und Praxis*, 2(59):91–99, 2008.

[58] Ingo Paulsen, Dominic Mainz, Katrin Weller, Indra Mainz, Jochen Kohl, and Arndt von Haeseler. Ontoverse: Collaborative Knowledge Management in the Life Sciences Network. In *Proceedings of the German e-Science Conference 2007 (GES 2007)*, May 2007.

[59] Helena Sofia Pinto and João P. Martins. Ontologies: How can they be built? *Knowledge and Information Systems*, 6:441–464, 2004. 10.1007/s10115-003-0138-1.

[60] Philip Resnik. Semantic Similarity in a Taxonomy: An Information-Based Measure and its Application to Problems of Ambiguity in Natural Language. *Journal of Artificial Intelligence Research*, 11:95–130, 1999.

[61] W. W. Royce. Managing the development of large software systems: concepts and techniques. In *Proceedings of the 9th international conference on Software Engineering*, ICSE '87, pages 328–338, Los Alamitos, CA, USA, 1987. IEEE Computer Society Press.

[62] G. Salton, A. Wong, and C. S. Yang. A vector space model for automatic indexing. *Commun. ACM*, 18(11):613–620, November 1975.

[63] Elena Simperl, Malgorzata Mochol, Tobias Brger, and Igor Popov. Achieving maturity: The state of practice in ontology engineering in 2009. In Robert Meersman, Tharam Dillon, and Pilar Herrero, editors, *On the Move to Meaningful Internet Systems: OTM 2009*, volume 5871 of *Lecture Notes in Computer Science*, pages 983–991. Springer Berlin / Heidelberg, 2009. 10.1007/978-3-642-05151-7_17.

[64] Katharina Siorpaes and Martin Hepp. Games with a purpose for the semantic web. *IEEE Intelligent Systems*, 23:50–60, 2008.

[65] S. Staab, R. Studer, H.-P. Schnurr, and Y. Sure. Knowledge processes and ontologies. *Intelligent Systems, IEEE*, 16(1):26 – 34, 2001.

[66] David Stephen and John Perrin. Prompt-viz: Ontology version comparison visualizations with treemaps. retrieved from http://webhome.cs.uvic.ca/~chisel/thesis/David_Perrin_Thesis.pdf, 2001.

[67] Rudi Studer, V. Richard Benjamins, and Dieter Fensel. Knowledge engineering: Principles and methods. *Data & Knowledge Engineering*, 25(1-2):161 – 197, 1998.

[68] Eiichi Sunagawa, Kouji Kozaki, Yoshinobu Kitamura, and Riichiro Mizoguchi. An environment for distributed ontology development based on dependency management. In Dieter Fensel, Katia P. Sycara, and John Mylopoulos, editors, *International Semantic Web Conference*, volume 2870 of *Lecture Notes in Computer Science*, pages 453–468. Springer, 2003.

[69] York Sure, Jürgen Angele, and Steffen Staab. OntoEdit: Multifaceted inferencing for ontology engineering. *Journal on Data Semantics*, LNCS(2800):128–152, 2003.

[70] York Sure, Michael Erdmann, Juergen Angele, Steffen Staab, Rudi Studer, and Dirk Wenke. Ontoedit: Collaborative ontology development for the semantic web. In *Proceedings of the first International Semantic Web Conference 2002, ISWC 2002" 2002*, Sardinia, Italia, June 9-12 2002. Springer, LNCS 2342.

[71] York Sure, Steffen Staab, and Rudi Studer. Methodology for development and employment of ontology based knowledge management applications. *SIGMOD Rec.*, 31:18–23, December 2002.

[72] B. Swartout, P. Ramesh, K. Knight, and T. Russ. Toward Distributed Use of Large-Scale Ontologies. *AAAI Symposium on Ontological Engineering*, 1997.

[73] Christoph Tempich, H. Sofia Pinto, and Steffen Staab. Ontology engineering revisited: an iterative case study. In *Proceedings of the 3rd European conference on The Semantic Web: research and applications*, ESWC'06, pages 110–124, Berlin, Heidelberg, 2006. Springer-Verlag.

[74] Christoph Tempich, Elena Simperl, Markus Luczak, Rudi Studer, and H. Sofia Pinto. Argumentation-based ontology engineering. *IEEE Intelligent Systems*, 22:52–59, 2007.

[75] Christoph Tempich, Elena Simperl, Markus Luczak, Rudi Studer, and H. Sofia Pinto. Argumentation-based ontology engineering. *IEEE Intelligent Systems*, 22:52–59, 2007.

[76] Tania Tudorache, Natalya Noy, Samson Tu, and Mark Musen. Supporting Collaborative Ontology Development in Protégé. In Amit Sheth, Steffen Staab, Mike Dean, Massimo Paolucci, Diana Maynard, Timothy Finin, and Krishnaprasad Thirunarayan, editors, *The Semantic Web - ISWC 2008*, volume 5318 of *Lecture Notes in Computer Science*, chapter 2, pages 17–32. Springer Berlin Heidelberg, Berlin, Heidelberg, 2010.

[77] Tania Tudorache and Natasha Noy. Collaborative protégé. In *Workshop on Social and Collaborative Construction of Structured Knowledge (CKC 2007) at WWW 2007*, Banff, Canada, 2007.

[78] Esko Ukkonen. Approximate string-matching with ¡italic¿q¡/italic¿-grams and maximal matches. *Theor. Comput. Sci.*, 92:191–211, January 1992.

[79] Mike Uschold. Building Ontologies: Towards a Unified Methodology. In *16th Annual Conf. of the British Computer Society Specialist Group on Expert Systems*, Cambridge, UK, 1996.

[80] Mike Uschold and Michael Grninger. Ontologies: principles, methods, and applications. *Knowledge Engineering Review*, 11(2):93–155, 1996.

[81] Mike Uschold and Martin King. Towards a methodology for building ontologies. In *Workshop on Basic Ontological Issues in Knowledge Sharing, held in conduction with IJCAI-95*, Montreal, Canada, 1995.

[82] Julio César Arpírez Vega, Óscar Corcho, Mariano Fernández-López, and Asunción Gómez-Pérez. Webode: a scalable workbench for ontological engineering. In *K-CAP*, pages 6–13. ACM, 2001.

[83] Max Völkel and Tudor Groza. Semversion: Rdf-based ontology versioning system. In *Proceedings of the IADIS International Conference WWW / Internet 2006 (ICWI 2006)*, 2006.

[84] Stefan Weinbrenner, Adam Giemza, and H. Ulrich Hoppe. Engineering heterogeneous distributed learning environments using tuple spaces as an architectural platform. In J. Michael Spector, Demetrios G. Sampson, Toshio Okamoto, Kinshuk, Stefano A. Cerri, Maomi Ueno, and Akihiro Kasihara, editors, *The 7th IEEE International Conference on Advanced Learning Technologies ICALT 2007*, pages 434–436, Los Alamitos, CA., 2007. IEEE Computer Society, IEEE Computer Society.

[85] Zhibiao Wu and Martha Palmer. Verb semantics and lexical selection. In *32nd. Annual Meeting of the Association for Computational Linguistics*, pages 133 –138, New Mexico State University, Las Cruces, New Mexico, 1994.

[86] Valentin Zacharias and Simone Braun. Soboleo – social bookmarking and lighweight engineering of ontologies. In Natalya Fridman Noy, Harith Alani, Gerd Stumme, Peter Mika, York Sure, and Denny Vrandecic, editors, *CKC*, volume 273 of *CEUR Workshop Proceedings*. CEUR-WS.org, 2007.

[87] Jürgen Ziegler Zoulfa El Jerroudi. Interaktives vergleichen und zusammenfuehren von ontologien. *i-com*, 6:44–49, 2007.